PUP

M000211470

THE OWNER'S HANDBOOK

SARA JOHN

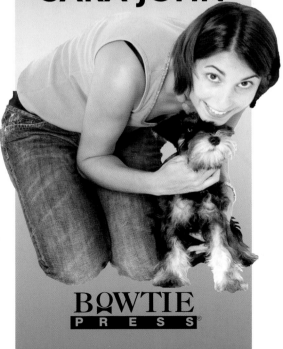

BOWTIE
P R E S S ®

First published in the USA and Canada
by BowTie Press
A Division of BowTie, Inc.
23172 Plaza Pointe Dr., Ste. 230
Laguna Hills, CA 92653
www.bowtiepress.com

Originally published in 2008 by Interpet
Publishing Ltd.

Library of Congress Cataloging-in-
Publication Data

John, Sara, 1954–
   The puppy pack : making the most of
puppy's first year / by Sara John.
      p. cm.
   ISBN 978-1-933958-27-9
   1. Puppies. I. Title.
   SF427.J55 2008
   636.7'07—dc22

2008029162

Copyright © 2009 by BowTie Press®

All rights reserved. No part of this book
may be reproduced, stored in a retrieval
system, or transmitted in any form or by
any means, electronic, mechanical, photo-
copying, recording, or otherwise, without
the prior written permission of BowTie
Press®, except for the inclusion of brief
quotations in an acknowledged review.

Printed and bound in China
12 11 10 09   1 2 3 4 5 6 7 8

The Author

Sara John realized her love of dogs at a very early age. She has been associated with dogs all her life, principally in three recognized breed groups, although she has also owned a variety of mutts. Her main love is the Soft Coated Wheaten Terrier, which she has owned, shown, and bred for over 25 years. During this time, her dogs have produced 14 litters, comprising a total of 86 puppies, and she has attended many dog shows, including Crufts, with her progeny. She is a Kennel Club–accredited judge for the breed in the United Kingdom.

Sara has earned a Diploma of Dog Breeding and Dog Judging, both with credit, and a Certificate in Canine Nutrition with the Animal Care College in Ascot. Lately, she has worked for the Animal Care College as a tutor and has furthered her own studies by passing Intermediate Canine Psychology and Advanced Canine Psychology.

She has held the position of Breed Club Secretary, more recently as a Committee Member and Match Secretary of Maidenhead District Canine Society, where dog owners are tutored on showing their dogs in the ring. She regularly participates in the annual Discover Dogs show at Earl's Court in London. While writing this book, Sara has undertaken her own extensive research based on her 25 years' experience of dog breeding. She has also conducted research with other Wheaten enthusiasts on *Playing With Your Dog*, published by the *Wheaten Health Initiative* newsletter, which has a worldwide distribution, and she has undertaken case study research on feeding dogs.

Acknowledgments

To my Dad, who loved dogs as much as I do. Thanks to Alun, my husband, and Guy and Lucy, my children. Also Dougal, Holly, Tessie, Bumpy, and Cracker. A special thanks goes to Smartie, who kept me company during many hours of writing!

CONTENTS

CHOOSING YOUR PUPPY

A well-trained dog provides a wonderful sense of companionship that is a real addition to any owner's life, and a dog offers tremendous benefits to his owner's health. Research shows that dog ownership leads to a significant decrease in serious health problems for some owners, and this has spurred volunteer groups to take dogs into senior citizens' homes and children's facilities.

We choose to keep dogs for many different reasons: for bringing an extra dimension to a family; for companionship; and for social, working, or security reasons. Dogs offer us the opportunity to exercise responsibility in a caring role because—no matter what our age—we find a real friend with whom it is good to share our time. Whatever your personal reasons for wanting a dog, this is the place to start when making the decision to acquire a dog.

Why Do You Want a Dog?

- Companionship
- Guarding your property
- Family playmate
- Showing, competing in agility, or as a walking companion
- Breeding a breed of dog that you particularly admire
- To fulfill a childhood wish
- As a working companion in a particular job
- Social reasons

You need to be clear exactly what you seek in dog ownership before taking on this responsibility. When humans and dogs live together, they create a mutual dependency. From our human point of view, dogs often take the place of a friend, child, or partner, and they seek to protect our homes; dogs, on the other hand, need the food, security, and social company we offer. Dogs, like us, convey messages using body language and facial expressions, but they do not have the advantages of verbal communication. Despite this constraint, dogs somehow learn to read all three types of communication. As good owners, humans need to understand natural dog behavior to learn how to socialize and train their dogs to behave sociably and be good canine citizens.

What Kind of Dog?

The type of dog that you choose is an important consideration. There are so many breeds, as well as mixed breeds or "mutts," and not all suit people in the right way, so a careful choice is essential.

Consider also whether a puppy or an older dog might better suit your circumstances or adapt better to a specific environment. You may adopt a dog needing a new home, but be aware that you must offer time and patience to organize some careful training for him to learn the new rules of behavior that suit your lifestyle.

Left: **All puppies are cute, but how do you choose the right one?**

Purebred or Mixed Breed?

Mixed breed or mutt	May have mixed parentage from a wide variety of different breeds, but the look of the dog may offer some insight into his origins and character.	Choices are made according to the information available from the rescue or shelter.
Sporting	Often identified as the easiest to train, with low aggression and outgoing demeanor. This is the most popular group; these breeds particularly enjoy family life.	Hunting, training, companionship. Have a reputation as making good family pets.
Non-sporting	Includes breeds of many different sizes, temperaments, and abilities.	Most make good family pets, but some may be more difficult to train.
Terrier	Have a tendency to dig. Bred for working and companionship; intelligent and very loyal. Like to be trained in short sharp bursts with constantly changing actions, or they lose interest. Can challenge family dynamics if jealousy occurs between two terriers.	Train in specific activities that appeal to the breed characteristics. Family dogs may be better if kept singly or as opposite-sex pairs.
Toy	Not always suitable for families with small children.	More suitable for small environments or for people not able to walk far.
Hound	Variety of sizes but all draw on their natural scenting ability or sight to hunt; many can run very fast and need plenty of exercise.	Mostly very gentle breeds, which may suit some families.
Working	Often draw on their natural instinct for guarding or working. Size is not consistent. All tend to be highly trainable but vary in reactivity and compatibility levels.	Ideal if you want a dog to train for activities.
Herding	Varieties mainly used for livestock herding; many different coats and temperaments.	Smart and trainable, as they will be more in touch with their natural behaviors.

Considering Your Circumstances

Consider why you want a dog. Is it to enjoy a more active
life, for your children, as a family addition, to guard your
home, to keep you healthy, for the activities it may entail,
or for other social reasons? Having identified your
primary motives, consider which would apply when
making your choice. This table may help you decide
which puppy would suit you best.

Purebred Dog	Mixed-breed Dog
• You will know size and nature of a breed	• Origin may be unknown
• May require more attention to health	• Usually very healthy
• Predictable features for each breed	• Often have unique features
• Characteristics predictable	• May be no indication of character
• Often knowledgeable breeders involved	• Background information may be sparse
• More expensive	• Within most people's budget

Large Dog	Small Dog
• May need large amounts of space	• Usually less space needed
• May need lots of exercise	• Exercise level may be comparable
• May need higher fences	• Limited or average containment needed
• Unsuitable for changing circumstances	• If circumstances change, may be easier
• Natural behaviors may be dominant	• Natural behaviors often easily managed
• Less likely to be tripped over or stepped on	• Small breeds may not suit family life
• Storage consideration for food	• Economical to feed

Male Dog	Female Dog
• Possibly stronger or more dominant	• More submissive with children
• May seek out female company	• Estrus occurs at regular intervals
• Marks his territory	• Urine stains the grass
• May be more protective of the home	• Possibly less territorial

Coat Type: Long	Coat Type: Short
• May require a lot of grooming	• Regular brushing to keep coat clean
• May need to learn how to trim	• Very little need to tidy coat if short
• More effort to bath the dog	• Occasional bath may be necessary
• Brings more dirt into the home	• Quick brush-down to remove debris
• May need cleaning after toileting	• Will be clean after toileting

Making an Informed Choice

- Puppies should look happy and healthy, with clean skin, ears, and eyes.
- Feces should be well formed and not loose.
- Gums should be a healthy pink, with teeth either formed or forming.
- The body should feel well fed and solid—not pot-bellied or fat.
- Puppies should take an interest in and respond to their surroundings.
- The dam at least should be present and allowed to join the litter as necessary.
- The kennel should be clean, airy, and light, with regular access to the yard.
- Pedigree papers and any health and vaccination records should be available for inspection.

Right: Rescue dogs come in all shapes and sizes, and they deserve a second chance.

Choosing an Older or Rescue Dog

Choose a reputable animal shelter or a breed club rescue group. Sometimes breeders have a puppy needing a home—perhaps one that is not suitable for showing or breeding or is a returned pet. Rescue groups obtain dogs from all sorts of places with many different reasons why each dog needs a good home. Ask lots of questions about them, and particularly about behaviors which may not suit your lifestyle or may create difficulties when retraining. The puppy may need to be house-trained, leash-trained, or trained to accept young or old family members or the presence of other dogs or other pets in his new home. Rescue dogs may come with their own sad life stories, but congratulate yourself if you take one on—you are giving your puppy or dog a second chance and a better life.

Expert Tip
- Always buy or adopt from a reputable breeder, rescue, or shelter.
- Follow up a personal recommendation, if possible.
- Find out as much as possible about the establishment.
- Study other animals at the same place, and buy only if you like what you see.

PUPPY PAPERWORK

Reputable breeders usually sell puppies with a receipt, a contract of sale, pedigree papers, copies of health records, and registration documents. It is your right to know the details and background of the litter before you purchase your puppy so you can look elsewhere if you choose.

Receipts are for money paid as a deposit and/or money paid at the time of collection. The contract is legally binding and identifies a sale between you and the breeder. Some breeders make personalized contracts with details relevant to them or to their particular breed. Usually two copies are provided, one for the owner and one for the breeder. A sample can be found on page 6 of *The Puppy Handbook* if you want an example for the breeder to complete.

The Contract and Conditions of Sale

Important details are the registered name of the puppy, date of birth, the breeder's name, and your details. The contract must include the price of the puppy, with any extras listed separately. If you wish to insure your puppy against theft or death, this contract will constitute a legal document stating the value of your puppy. The date of purchase will be given for insurance coverage to start. You should also be given a receipt for a puppy adopted from a rescue or shelter for estimating his value for insurance purposes.

Make sure your puppy is healthy by visiting your chosen vet for an initial check-up within two weeks of bringing him home. Once the puppy leaves his kennel, the breeder may not accept responsibility if you seek compensation for problems arising months later, which might have been noticed at a much earlier date. Resolving problems at the start allows you either to negotiate a replacement puppy or to get your money back before you become too attached to the new arrival.

Specific points relating to any health checks may be included in the contract if you intend to breed your puppy. Personalized details may be added, such as the recommendation that owners seeking to breed their dogs should obtain advice first, and it may state that the breeder does not accept responsibility for your mistakes. Responsible breeders often include a clause ensuring that unwanted dogs are returned to them.

Breeders may sell certain pups with a limited registration to prevent litters from being

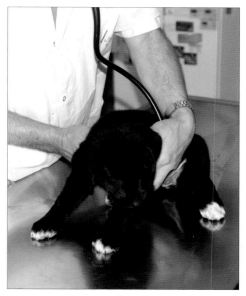

Above: **Taking your puppy to the vet early on ensures good health from the start.**

registered, to prohibit showing or breeding if specific faults or inherited defects are obvious, or relating to exporting the dog to another country. In a personalized contract of sale, breeders decide what clauses they wish to impose.

Signing the Contract

Contracts should conclude with a signature provided by both parties and include an address for each party as well as the date the contract was exchanged. Each party retains a copy for the dog's records, which may also include any pedigree restrictions, health certificates relating to your puppy, and any relevant screening results for the whole litter. If a health check relates to litter screening, individual puppies should be identified by the breeder. By doing this, you are able to specifically identify that your puppy has had some health checks completed, and you will know what may need repeating if a restriction is to be lifted in the future for breeding purposes.

Purebred puppies are usually (but not always) registered as a litter with the American Kennel Club (AKC) by the breeder. The breeder should then supply an individual registration application to each puppy buyer. The new owner then submits the completed application and the registration fee to the AKC, which will mail out the pup's registration certificate. Registration documents detail the pedigree name, registration number, and the line of parentage. Also included will be details of eye tests, hearing tests, and blood tests, as well as orthopedic scores (that is, hip scores) if the parents have been scored by a registering organization.

Below: Each puppy in a litter should have documentation recording its kennel name, registration number, and any health checks completed.

Checklist of Important Paperwork
- Contract of sale
- Registration documents
- Pedigree
- Health records
- Receipt
- Insurance policy (if this is included in the sale)

Left: A puppy for sale should be well fed, have pink gums, and look healthy. The nose should be cold and the eyes bright and clear.

9

What's in a Pedigree?

Purebred puppies are usually sold with "papers," which may be unfamiliar to you. The pedigree and the AKC registration details are two of the most important. The pedigree means that your puppy has been carefully bred and that the breeder is allowing you the opportunity and the privilege of sharing the pride he has taken in producing good dogs.

Registration with the AKC endorses this if the puppy is registered and provides a formal identity document at the time of purchase. AKC-certified pedigrees are three or four generations long. They list each dog's registered name and any titles, registration number, coat color, and date of entry into the Stud Book.

The breeder will probably give you your puppy's pedigree attached to the contract. It will detail the sires and dams at each generation antecedent to your puppy. It will also list, where applicable, health certification numbers such as those from Orthopedic Foundation for Animals or the Canine Eye Registration Foundation, indicating health clearances for those dogs.

Having champions or field trial champions in a pedigree does not guarantee that a puppy will be healthy, of good temperament, a future champion, or well behaved! Championship status and good behavior will be achieved only by your hard work, time, and a great deal of patience.

Most successful dogs have earned their championships by applying hours of hard work and determination. Dogs may have been campaigned at shows for many years to win the points necessary to achieve this status. An AKC champion needs to earn 15 points at shows under at least three different judges, including two "majors" of three or more points under two different judges. This involves a great deal of training and travel.

Abbreviations You May Find in Your Puppy's Pedigree

Prefixes:

Ch. *(Champion)* Indicates the dog has been made a champion in his own country.

Ch. preceded by the abbreviation of a country's name Indicates that the dog is a champion in that country, e.g., Can. Ch. (Canadian Champion), Eng. Ch. (English Champion), Mex. Ch. (Mexican Champion), etc.

DC *(Dual Champion)* Indicates that the dog has earned the Ch. title as well as either the Field Champion (FC) or Herding Champion (HC) title.

Int. Ch. *(International Champion)* Indicates that the dog is a champion in several countries.

Suffixes:

CD *(Companion Dog)* Indicates three qualifying scores under three different judges in the Novice class of obedience.

JE *(Junior Earthdog)* Indicates qualification at two Junior Earthdog tests under two different judges.

NA *(Novice Agility)* Indicates three qualifying scores under two different judges at the Novice level of agility.

RN *(Rally Novice)* Indicates three qualifying scores under two different judges in the Novice class of rally.

Of course, these are just a few of the basic titles that a dog can earn. The AKC alone offers close to 100 titles in more than a dozen areas of canine competition.

Affixes or Kennel Names

The kennel name will appear as part of the pup's registered name. For example, the author's dogs all have the affix Dohoci. The author's current two dogs are officially registered as Dohoci Talulah and Dohoci Kiss'N'Tell. Occasionally a dog may carry the kennel name at the end as a suffix. For example, a dog purchased from elsewhere may

Below: **A solid pedigree and plenty of time spent socializing and training your puppy will pay dividends for a family dog.**

Above: **A pedigree full of champions gives no guarantee of future temperament, social behavior, or good health. These depend on good feeding and time spent playing, training, and socializing your puppy.**

have "of Dohoci" added at the end of the registered name, which indicates ownership within that kennel but that the dog has been bred elsewhere.

Breeders can apply to register their kennel names with the AKC. This protects the usage of the name by other breeders. In order to gain registration for his kennel name, a breeder must meet requirements regarding participation in AKC events, adherence to the AKC's ethical breeding policies, and the number of registered litters bred in a given time frame. The breeder must fill out the application and provide documentation of these activities to have his request for kennel name registration considered by the AKC. The application is reviewed and, if registration is granted, it must be renewed every five years or else the name will be released for public use.

EQUIPMENT YOU WILL NEED

Dog beds—Use cardboard boxes initially, as baskets can be chewed, soiled, or generally vandalized! But various bed styles, sizes, and shapes are available. You may need a larger size later.

- Wicker baskets: Can be difficult to clean, are easily chewed, and pieces easily swallowed. They creak slightly during movement, which may comfort a puppy!
- Plastic baskets: Can be chewed and may leave sharp spikes if chewing is regular, causing injury. Easy to clean, last a lifetime, and are draft-proof, important for young or elderly dogs. Require a washable blanket or fleece.
- Soft fabric beds, bean bags: Washable, chewable, soft, and comfortable.

- Crate: You may prefer a crate suitable for your puppy to sleep in or for training purposes.

Blankets—Blankets can probably be found around your home, in thrift stores, and the like. They should be washable, soft with no edges to chew or swallow easily, and placed over a thick layer of newspaper. Dog fleeces are useful because they offer one-way moisture reduction in the event that your puppy urinates in the bed.

Pen—For containment at night or when home alone; pens limit the area in which your puppy can roam for safety and house-training purposes. A bed inside is required.

Water and food bowls—Choose small bowls initially, changing to an appropriate size later.

- Pottery: Washable and usually too heavy to knock around! They become porous with long-term use and break if dropped. Soak in very diluted bleach, then wash thoroughly to remove the slimy feel that can develop even if washed regularly. More expensive to buy.
- Metal: Washable, unbreakable, and easily packed for travel. No matter how old they are, they still look good. They can mark teeth slightly if your puppy picks them up. Medium-priced to expensive, depending on the quality.
- Plastic: Ideal for very young puppies but not suitable to be left down on the floor, as they frequently act as a toy substitute. Very chewable, they can cause problems if pieces break off and are swallowed, so they should be thrown away before this happens. Washable, light, cheap, and easily packed for a day out or a vacation.

Newspaper—Start saving your papers before your puppy arrives, as you will need a large supply for paper-training! After a while, move the paper outside to encourage your puppy to understand that toileting is an outside activity! Use large sheets of newspaper, which are absorbent and cover a greater area.

Above: **Always buy a crate that allows room for your puppy to grow into it.**

Expert Tip
Some people keep collars and leashes for subsequent puppies because the items wear very little during the time they are used. Ask around; someone may lend you a set for a short while. The puppy requires a permanent one with an ID tag once he is old enough to go out.

Safety Tips
- Never leave your puppy alone in the car.
- Secure your puppy on a collar and leash in areas that are not safely enclosed.
- Ask your vet about when your pup will have received the proper vaccinations to go out and about.
- Have proper identification for your pup.

Harnesses are useful for securing your puppy for car travel.

Food—The breeder may provide some food but should also give you dietary advice before you collect your puppy. Check out local pet shops before picking the puppy up, and try to find the most knowledgeable supplier. Some may give a discount for bulk buying.

Collars—There is a wide choice available: leather, chain, rope, or nylon; flat, rolled, two-ply; buckle or snap closure. A soft collar is best until your puppy gets used to it around his neck. Long-haired dogs benefit from a rolled or soft collar to prevent their hair from tearing under the material. Other breeds may benefit from large, wide collars. Avoid chain collars on your puppy, although they are still sometimes used on adult dogs of certain breeds. The breeder or pet shop can give advice if you are unsure. All collars must fit correctly and have a metal identity tag attached. Very rarely, an allergic reaction can occur caused by the dye used to color leather collars.

Leads—Can be made of leather, rope, nylon, or chain and in a variety of weights and lengths to suit different breeds and owners. Flexible leashes extend a distance from a plastic carrying handle and are useful for walking in areas near roads, as they keep the dog close to you.

Body harnesses—These are useful to stop your puppy from pulling when out walking and to secure your puppy safely in the car for traveling. Use a harness or a crate every time you travel by car, even for short journeys. Do be careful if using them on some breeds or if your puppy does pull a lot, as they can increase muscle around the shoulder area. If your puppy is to be shown, it may unbalance the conformation of the dog if the shoulders are "loaded."

Dog coats—Some breeds (such as Whippets) feel the cold more, so ask the breeder's advice as to using a coat or sweater for dogs.

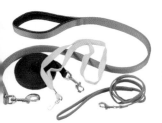

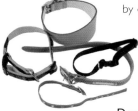

Above: **Collars and leashes come in many different types and sizes and must fit correctly.**

Other Useful Equipment

Grooming kit—Be guided by the breeder regarding long-haired dogs, as some breeds require specific grooming and tidying regimens that you may need to learn. Pet dogs require only basic items, which can be used with your puppy standing on the ground or on a table. Short-haired dogs benefit from brushing, as this also gives you time to complete regular health check-ups and encourages familiarity with handling. The breeder may have already started gentle grooming with your puppy or taught him to stand still on a table, so do ask how this was done.

Checklist of Useful Grooming Kit Items

Brushes: Appropriate shapes and sizes for the coat type.

Combs: Different sizes, with or without handles, and with fine or wide teeth spacing.

Special combs: Dematting comb, shedding comb, flea comb types.

Scissors: Different types do different things—some have fine blades, some are used for thinning, and others have curved ends for cutting closer to certain body parts.

Electric clippers: For removing large areas of coat and for thinning.

Nail clippers: For clipping the nails.

Tweezers: For debris removal (seeds between toes or ear hair plucking).

Bathing items: Shampoo, conditioners, and hair dryers per specific breed needs.

Teeth-cleaning kit: A soft canine toothbrush or finger brush and special dog-friendly toothpaste. Teeth-cleaning treats are useful but do not keep the teeth as clean.

Towels, paper towels, poop bags, poop scoop for the yard: These can be obtained while doing your general shopping or found among household items around your home.

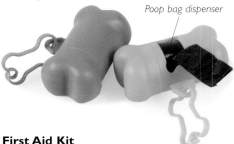

Poop bag dispenser

First Aid Kit

Some basic items, such as a suitable canine antiseptic wash, antiseptic cream, and a selection of bandages and dressings are useful. If you are going on vacation with your puppy, remember to include your home address or contact details in case of an emergency.

Choosing Toys

A variety of different shapes and sizes of toys may be desirable; some may suit certain breeds more than others, depending on their characteristics. Dog chews—while not really intended as toys—can be included in the selection, as these also provide stimulus for the dog's natural behavior. The main rule regarding the choice of any toy or chew stick should be safety and enjoyment, particularly if your puppy is to achieve satisfaction from the item if left for any period of time to play on his own. Some chew sticks are colored with an edible dye, which may stain fur or fabrics. Put the

Right: **Rawhide chews are alternatives to toys and acceptable chew items for teething puppies.**

Above: **Choose toys for your puppy that are safe to play with or to chew.**

toys away at the end of playtime to avoid the risk of tripping over them.

Check the following when you buy toys:

- No sharp edges that could damage your puppy's soft mouth or erupting teeth.
- Make sure toys with small parts cannot be chewed so as to cause the parts to come off, after which they may be swallowed.
- Do not give a small ball to a large breed of dog, as he may swallow it and choke.
- Do not give a large ball to a small dog, as he may injure himself trying to play with it.
- Do not allow your puppy to play with children's toys, as many are not as indestructible as properly manufactured dog toys are.
- If you give a rawhide chew to use as a toy, make sure your puppy does not ingest any

chewed-off pieces, which could get stuck in his throat.

- If you give your puppy old boxes to chew or sleep in, make sure there are no staples that might be chewed or swallowed. Cardboard paper-roll tubes or egg crates are safer.
- Do not give plastic bottles, as these can shred into pieces and get stuck in the dog's throat.

The list below was recommended as favorite toys by a group of experienced owners:

Rags	Large rope toy
Pull toys	Hard rope
Noisy toys	Soft rope
Soft toys	Rubber ring
Hard rubber toy	Frisbee
Teething toys	Stuffed toys
Ball	Empty small boxes
Old football	Solitaire block toy
Spiky dog ball	Old socks
Teddy bears	Nylon dog bones
Furry toys	Filled bones
Squeaky toys	Squeaky plastic bones

Right: **The variety of toys available can seem over-whelming to new owners. Choose two or three to start, and then add a few more as your puppy grows and needs more stimulation or different games to play with you.**

WELCOMING YOUR PUPPY HOME

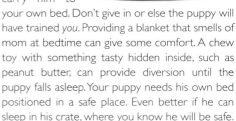

Start to establish routines to help your puppy get to know what typically happens around the house and when. A routine will have been established by the breeder around mealtimes, so it may be easier to stick with this and fit your own life around this timetable initially. You also need time to house-train, socialize, and exercise your puppy and find time to play together when he is awake to start his early training. The early months of having a puppy are usually the busiest because there is so much to learn.

Working families should establish a routine from the first day. If you have a dog sitter, invite her to learn this routine, see where food and equipment is kept, and give a feeding or two. Provide work telephone numbers and veterinary details in case of an emergency, and discuss your wishes in the event of different scenarios. Involve family members and your dog sitter with your puppy's training so you are all consistent, as any bad habits the puppy may learn from other handlers will imprint on his mind. Certain behaviors learned early on may be appealing, but they can lead to greater problems down the line. Prevention from day one is easier than having to retrain your dog later.

Time for Bed

A set routine is vital when leaving your puppy alone or at bedtime. Getting your puppy to settle down the first few nights requires some patience and good judgment. A puppy will whine and whimper the first night in an attempt to persuade you to pick him up and carry him to your own bed. Don't give in or else the puppy will have trained *you*. Providing a blanket that smells of mom at bedtime can give some comfort. A chew toy with something tasty hidden inside, such as peanut butter, can provide diversion until the puppy falls asleep. Your puppy needs his own bed positioned in a safe place. Even better if he can sleep in his crate, where you know he will be safe.

Some people allow pets to sleep beside their beds. This allows you to take your puppy out during the night if he needs to relieve himself. It is recommended that you cover the area with an old piece of carpet or with newspaper that can be thrown away when house-training is complete. If your puppy sleeps next to you at night, he should be enclosed in his crate or you should have your bedroom door closed so he cannot wander throughout the house.

Below: **Paper-train your puppy to encourage clean habits at night.**

House-training

House-training passes through several stages, from the first hours after birth until your puppy is clean indoors. At birth, the dam licks the puppy's tummy to stimulate elimination and keep the bed clean. When the litter starts moving, she does this when they leave the bed so they make the association of leaving the bed with gaining her attention for their bodily needs. Once they are eliminating without this stimulation, they learn to leave the bed and usually seek the area farthest away from their bed in which to toilet. Most breeders will put newspaper down to catch this, and hence your puppy may be paper-trained already when you pick him up.

Personal experience has shown that puppies as young as six weeks old will run to an open back door and do their business outside if given the opportunity. It is this association you must try to harness if house-training is to be quick and relatively successful. Nighttimes will remain messy for some time because puppies do not have the capacity or control to last for several hours without toileting until they are at least a few months old. Some breeds may achieve this

earlier, while others may take longer, and bitches may take longer than dogs. Whatever time it takes, your puppy will succeed more quickly if you are vigilant and patient.

Good routine involves regular visits outside during the day and putting newspaper on the floor at night for accidents; this will create less mess for you to clean up the following morning. Keep a safe cleaning agent and a mop handy for the first few weeks. If you're crate-training your pup, he may whine or cry at night to be taken out. Don't ignore him! Get out of bed and take him out to instill good habits. Keep reminding your puppy where his toilet area is and reward him if you see him being good.

Your puppy may release drops of urine when he is excited. This is normal, and as your puppy's skills improve and he becomes more socialized and used to various events going on around him, this will stop. If it does continue into maturity, you should get this problem checked out by your vet.

Below: **Involve all the family, including children, with your puppy's training so that he learns to respect and trust human contact.**

Establishing Those Important Ground Rules

Your puppy needs to learn the boundaries of his relationship with you. You are his leader in all things, and your puppy must quickly learn to respect this.

Off-limits areas—You may wish to establish off-limits areas in your home, either for reasons of hygiene or, more important, to stop other problems from developing. For instance, you cannot know what your puppy is up to if you cannot see him. Your puppy could get into mischief chewing electrical cords, running off with toilet paper, or chewing the children's treasured toys or school shoes. Teach your dog which areas are permissible to enter and how he should behave. Stretching the boundaries too wide can lead to a puppy's developing a greater level of independence, which you may prefer to discourage. Decide on the areas, and stick to them when your puppy arrives. Trying to impose restrictions later on after your puppy has established his territory is harder.

Furniture—Climbing on the furniture is not recommended because of the risk of falling. If your puppy is not to be allowed on furniture, be consistent about keeping your puppy off. Gently push him down and say "No."

Jumping up—No matter how adorable it seems, train your puppy not to! Gently push the puppy down and say "Good dog" in a gentle, kind tone when his paws are back on the floor.

Establishing Yourself as Top Dog

Your puppy needs to learn this, so establish yourself as his leader from the beginning.

Do:
- Make your puppy walk behind you when going through doorways.
- Eat your meals before feeding your puppy.
- Teach your puppy to allow you to take away his toys or food.
- Sit in your puppy's bed occasionally to establish your rights over his space.

Don't:
- Let your puppy into the house just because he barks.
- Feed your puppy on demand.
- Let your puppy misbehave and not correct him immediately.
- Let your puppy become possessive about his possessions.

Naming Your Puppy

You may have names ready for your puppy before he arrives, or you may not. Books to help you choose are available. Include all family members, and aim to select a name that is not difficult or embarrassing to use. Choose short, sharp, one- or two-syllable names, such as Rex or Holly. Introduce your puppy to his name, and use it for all training exercises. If you already have a dog or cat, choose a different-sounding name for your new puppy. The pup's name will be needed for his health records, so it makes sense to choose it fairly quickly as soon as your puppy arrives home, before your first vet visit.

The breeder may have started calling the litter collectively for feeding times. If so, for the first few days use the phrase "Puppy, (chosen name) puppy." After a few days, drop one "Puppy," then after another few days drop the second, using only your chosen name. By doing so, your puppy quickly learns that when a command is given, he must respond. For example, the command "Smartie, sit" may evoke more response than just "Sit" because your puppy learns that the order is intended for him.

Picking Up and Holding Your Puppy

Young animals will struggle if picked up and can be easily dropped, so initially discourage children from handling them. Hold your puppy gently and securely, talking in reassuring tones without causing alarm. Hold him with one hand under the chest (or brisket) and between the front legs, and the other hand supporting the rear. Large puppies are best held across and around the chest and rear using both arms. *Never* lift a puppy by the scruff of his neck, as this causes pain and injury. Most dogs don't mind being picked up if they are familiar with being held, but be careful if the dog is upset or seems aggressive.

Discourage children from holding your puppy unless under supervision. Sit a child on the floor cross-legged. Place your puppy in his lap and, using distraction, encourage your puppy to sit quietly. Encourage stroking

Above: **Hold your puppy gently and securely with both hands.**
Left: **Sit children on the floor cross-legged to hold a puppy.**

or soothing if the puppy struggles. Encourage the child to sit quietly without shouting or making a lot of noise, and make gentle conversation to stop your puppy from feeling frightened. Never allow grabbing at your puppy, picking him up, or pushing him around. This would simply encourage snapping or snarling if your puppy is fearful of being hurt.

Encourage your puppy to sit quietly.

Introducing New Family Members

Introducing a new family member can distress other pets, especially if a dog has been the sole beneficiary of his owner's affections for some time.

This can relate to the arrival of a new baby, elderly relatives moving in, or even the arrival of a  new puppy. Problems occur if the dog is not pretrained to expect changes, particularly as introducing a new baby is probably the most important event in any family's life.

Loss of attention— Prior to any new arrival, existing dogs can be taught to accept less attention for increasingly longer periods of time. Avoid giving them attention or physical contact at certain times or on demand, and initiate contact only at convenient times and places. It is good for dogs to learn to spend some part of the day away from the owner in another part of the house, so early familiarity with being left alone can be started when young. For advice on introducing a new puppy to an existing dog, see *The Puppy Handbook*, page 22.

Introducing a new baby—An empty baby seat can help familiarize your puppy with this item if placed on the floor. Early training should include using suitable commands such as "Leave it" or "Stay" when your puppy approaches it. Clicker training or providing rewards at regular intervals for appropriate behaviors is essential. Practice with an old blanket on the carpet and one or two toys, and use "Leave it," "Stay," or "Move" when your puppy shows interest. Your puppy must understand that he is not allowed on the rug.

Once your puppy is used to the baby equipment, place a doll in different items, such as the baby seat or stroller. The same process of teaching the dog to leave it should be used, but allow him time to smell the doll, and reward your puppy for appropriate behavior. Discourage your puppy from licking or nosing, and reward him when he leaves the doll alone. Leaving your puppy alone with the doll as a trial may give you an indication of the reaction you can expect. If your puppy tips the chair over or generally takes too much interest, return immediately and train your puppy to leave it. If the dog is frightened by these consequences, entice him back to a state of calm and reduce his stress.

Gradual familiarization—At frequent intervals, playing a recording of a crying baby will familiarize your puppy and interest him, so reward appropriate behavior. This noise should be played upstairs (loudly) so your puppy gets used to the

Below: **Puppies coexist happily with new babies if trained in what to expect and how to behave.**

Offer treats held in a cupped hand.

Above: **Teaching children how to feed treats to a puppy properly can prevent snatching later.**

noise coming from different parts of the house. Use the clicker or lure and reward (see pages 50–51) for distraction, and teach the puppy to accept the sound quietly.

Regularly each day, cuddle the doll and talk to it with members of your family, ignoring your puppy if he intervenes. Carrying the doll around or placing it in a high chair are ways of getting your puppy used to a baby's presence. Eventually, when your puppy is familiar with this, invite a friend with a baby (one who lives with dogs) to the house. Allow your puppy to smell and watch you feeding and talking to the infant.

When your baby arrives, allow your puppy to smell him or her, and offer a soiled diaper to sniff. Don't forget that your puppy also needs his turn for love and attention. However, keep the baby away as much as possible initially, and introduce him or her as part of your routine. If your puppy has responded to training, he will behave as though the

Right: **Correct bonding and safe handling develop lifelong friendships between children and family dogs.**

baby is part of the family. These methods were used by the author personally when starting a family, and they worked very well.

Health and Safety Issues for Young Children

- *Never* leave your children or their friends and your puppy in the same room unsupervised. Instruct your puppy to leave the room and let him return only with you.
- Discourage feeding your puppy at the table, as that may encourage a tendency to steal food or beg. Never leave dogs and babies unsupervised at mealtimes, and always separate multiple dogs at their mealtimes or when given bones.
- Worm your puppy regularly if you have children in the family.
- If your puppy does not tolerate your family well, you must consider the risks of allowing him to remain with your family. Consider whether retraining your puppy will be a possibility or whether it may be kinder to rehome him.
- Organize a routine for your family that allows you to devote some of your time to your puppy; he will soon get fed up with always being left out of what you are doing. Take your puppy on outings, and do not leave him home alone for long periods because this may cause separation anxiety and jealousy toward the children.
- Teach your children when and how to give your puppy treats.
- In the event of a fire, put your puppy on a leash, take him outside, and supervise him as you would your children. Do not let him run around in panic, preventing you or your family from evacuating the area.

DIET AND NUTRITION

The early ancestors of your puppy probably ate rumen (stomachs of ruminants) and organs from their prey, with the addition of seasonal berries, grains, and grass. Although dogs are carnivores, they also eat vegetables. The fact that dog food today bears little resemblance to food eaten in the wild is why some health and behavioral problems are associated with incorrect diets.

Your puppy should experience different foods in the early days for his proper growth and development; he should not survive on meat alone. Supermarket brands of food are an option, but a dog's nutritional requirements include vegetables, meats, supplements, and the nutrients needed for survival and healthy development.

A balanced diet contains:

- Protein—for maintenance, for growth, and to regulate body metabolism.
- Carbohydrates—converts to glucose for energy metabolism.
- Fat—essential fatty acids maintain skin and coat and provide energy.
- Minerals and vitamins—for bone formation and development and blood chemistry.
- Fiber—to support the digestive function.

In the correct combination, these promote good bone growth with correct skeletal development and maintenance for the adult dog. Food must include suitable elements for your individual puppy (his size, activity level, and body requirements) and be acceptable in terms of cost, supply, and storage requirements.

Proportions must be correctly balanced for size and activity. Certain types of food may influence brain activity, affect all-around behavior, and disrupt learning. Manipulating the balance of dietary chemicals can aid in learning or behavior problems, but this should not be necessary if the correct guidelines are used. If food-related problems do occur, you should seek professional help to make diet changes, or you may risk missing essential nutrients from the diet.

Water is the other essential element. Water makes up most of your puppy's body weight and influences biochemical reactions in the body. Your puppy cannot sustain life without drinking large quantities, so provide fresh water daily. Water is found in varying amounts in most dog food but not much is found in dry foods. The more water in the food, the less your puppy will drink from his bowl.

Choosing from the Options

The choices of food include wet, semi-moist, frozen, dry kibble, and a natural or mixed diet. Not all dogs have similar requirements, hence the many types of food included in this list. Breed, size, health status, daily habits, working or companion jobs, and the personal preferences of owners or breeders all provide individual reasons why dogs differ in both their feeding habits and their nutritional needs.

What Choices Are Available?

Wet Food	Canned	• Contains meat and by-products. • Some contain only 4 percent meat base. • Usually contain up to 80 percent water. • Can be mixed with dry food. • Supposedly lower incidence of allergies. • Digestion takes around nine hours. • Check carefully for a balanced diet. • Bulky to store. • Cannot be left out in dog's bowl.
	Sealed semi-moist packs	• Similar to canned, but usually more meat. • The food is not sterilized in packaging. • Stabilized with preservatives.
	Frozen	• 100 percent meat or animal parts included. • Requires a mixer. • Used with vegetables for a natural diet. • Must be kept in freezer. • Needs defrosting before use.
Dry Food	Kibble	• Contains animal by-products. • Many contain around 20 percent meat base. • Convenient and clean to serve. • Free access to bowl as dog requires. • Brand leaders available worldwide. • Can be used as training treats. • Digestion takes around 16 hours. • Less fecal output.
Natural/Mixed Diets	Diet of raw meat, vegetables, and bones	• Homemade with fresh/frozen meat. • Variety of vegetables to prepare. • Adding vitamins and minerals is essential. • More time-consuming to prepare. • Digestion takes around six hours. • Reduced allergies and digestive problems. • Many benefits to health. • Less fecal output.

Other Considerations When Selecting a Diet

Cost: Cheaper brands have reduced quality and use fillers to enhance or bulk up a product. Certain by-products of meat, such as feathers, hooves, and horns, may be included. There is nothing wrong with a cheaper variety providing it suits your dog. Take advice on which type of feeding regimen suits your puppy, but review the quality frequently. Some foods may require mixers or fillers to be added.

Storage—Look at space for storage in the kitchen, shed, or garage if you shop for large quantities of food. Store correctly and use by the recommended date to maintain the quality of the food, and beware of rodents or other pests.

Purchasing—Dry or frozen food is frequently purchased in bulk, involving a trip to the pet shop. Canned food, raw meat, and vegetables can be

Left: Hard biscuits or nylon bones can serve to keep your puppy amused. As he chews, they also help clean plaque off the teeth.

purchased weekly in smaller quantities. Specific food may be difficult to get when on vacation.

Logistics—Plan what to feed your dog on vacation, either taking provisions with you or finding out if you can buy your brand locally. Dry food may be easier to feed but not so easy to store. Canned food is easier to store, but cans need to be disposed of properly. Traveling abroad may be easier with dry food because of its worldwide availability.

Ease of serving—Large bags can be heavy, and unused canned food must be covered and refrigerated. Anyone who looks after your dog must know how to properly serve correct portions and store the food.

Hygiene—Wet food attracts flies on hot days. Bowls can become encrusted with dried food, allowing bacteria to thrive. This can be difficult to remove, but soaking the bowl in a solution of very weak bleach (a few drops in a basin of water will do) before washing will help.

Food labels on cans and packages—Labels can be open to misinterpretation in terms of the quantity necessary to feed, thus resulting in obesity at a relatively early age. Many labels recommend an amount within an upper and lower range, so owners must judge for themselves if the quantity given is excessive, just right, or insufficient. There is a formula to figure out calorie intake.

Above: **Plan ahead for vacations. Think about your puppy's feeding arrangements, where he will sleep, and what equipment you will need.**

Estimating the Calorie Requirements for Different Breeds

Weight range of dog (lb.)		Calories required in food	Breed examples
Small	5	200	Chihuahua, Pomeranian
	10	350	Mini Dachshund
	15	450	Parson Russell Terrier
Medium	20	575	Beagle
	30	775	Cocker Spaniel
	40	975	Brittany, Bulldog
Large	50	1150	Pointer
	70	1475	Labrador
	80+	1625 and up	Bloodhound, Newfoundland

This is easier to estimate with labeled fresh foods, but you can use the following formula with others:

Canned food example—Supermarket Chunks in Gravy (400g).

The label says this food contains:

Crude Protein = 8% *(x 4 = 32) Protein contains 4 calories per gram*

Crude Fat = 5% *(x 9= 45) Fat contains 9 calories per gram*

Crude Fiber = 0.5%

Moisture = 80% *(i.e., 20% is dry matter)*

Ash = 2.2%

Total = **95.7%** *(100% - 95.7% = 4.3% nitrogen free extract or NFE)*

Using the formula of 4.3 (NFE) x 4 (protein calories) = 17.2, add 28 (protein), add 42.5 (fat) = 87.7 x 100 for calorie value

Calorie content = **877 calories per kg, or 351 calories per 400g can.**

To ascertain the exact amount of protein, divide the stated protein content (8%) by the dry matter content (20%) and multiply by 100: 8/20 x 100 = 40%. In reality, this food contains more protein than stated on the label and may not suit certain age groups or dogs with health problems.

Always provide quality food for your growing puppy.

Changing the Breeder's Recommended Diet

A daily diet sheet should be provided by the breeder, and in some cases even food for a few days. If you want to change the diet, wait until your puppy has settled in and then:

- review all the products available from local sources;
- discuss ideas with other people who own the same breed;
- ensure that the basic nutritional requirements are met, and change the diet slowly;
- check that the correct amount of nutrition and calories are in the new food.

The breeder should complete the Diet Sheet provided in *The Puppy Handbook* (page 39), but do use it to make your own if you need to, using the information from this section. Evaporated milk used is diluted in proportions of one part milk to two parts water. Water must be accessible at all times.

Vitamins and supplements, recommended by the breeder or obtained from the pet store, should be added following the directions on the package according to age and/or size. Seasonal oils (salmon, linseed, cod liver) may be added in small quantities according to the size of the dog, as these provide essential fatty oils that keep the skin and coat in good condition. Some oils may be unsuitable for the breed if the coat is not meant to be soft.

Example of a mixed-food diet for a medium-size dog—adult size 35 to 45 lb.

	7:00 a.m.	12:00 p.m.	3:00 p.m.	7:00 p.m.	Bedtime
On collection	I scrambled egg, I Tbsp oatmeal with diluted milk	2 oz. raw meat & a little chopped vegetable, with ¼ cup prepared oatmeal	2 Tbsp prepared oatmeal	⅓ can of puppy food and ¼ cup prepared oatmeal	¼ pint diluted milk
12 weeks	As above	As above	As above	As above	As above
4 – 6 months	As above	Increase to 3.5 oz. raw meat and veg. and raise oatmeal to ½ cup	As above	Increase to ½ can of puppy food and ½ cup oatmeal	Stop
6 – 9 months	Replace this meal with 12 p.m. meal, can replace meat with ¾ can	Stop		Change to an adult canned food, increasing to ¾ can and ½ cup oatmeal	
12 months	As above	Stop	Stop	Increase to I can	

Homemade diet for a medium-size adult dog fed twice daily

Only one or two choices of meat should be given daily. The correct caloric value and quantity given is essential.

Food	Caloric content	Daily frequency	Contains
Beef mince—raw	400 cal per 4.5 oz.	2 to 3 times weekly, 3.5 oz. per meal	Protein, fat, vitamins B, B2, B6, D, phosphorus, potassium, copper
Lamb mince—raw	250 cal per 3.5 oz.	2 to 3 times weekly, 3.5 oz. per meal	Protein, vitamin B12, various minerals
Sardines	250 cal per 4 oz. can	I can, once weekly	Vitamin A, B6, iodine
Chicken mince—raw or cooked	Approx 250 cal (accounting for cooking)	2 to 3 times weekly, 4 oz. per meal	Protein, fat, vitamin B, minerals
Chicken wings—raw	I75 per 3 oz.	I to 3 times weekly, 3 oz. each	Calcium, protein, phosphorus, magnesium
Marrow bone	According to % of fat in the marrow	Once weekly	Calcium, copper, fat, phosphorus, magnesium, protein
Tripe—raw	About 25 cal per oz.	Twice weekly, 7 oz. per meal	Folic acid, biotin, pantothenic acid, protein, fat
Canned food	Average of 342 cal per I4 oz. can	Twice weekly, 7 oz. per meal	Will vary; see label
Oatmeal–instant (prepared)	80 cal per ½ cup	2 to 3 times weekly	Fiber, carbohydrate, protein, fat
Biscuit treats	I6 to 20 cal for 3	3 biscuits (.25 oz. each)	Carbohydrate
Chopped mixed vegetables	Negligible	Daily	Vitamins A, B, B6, E, K, iron, iodine
Carrot or apple, grated	50 cal per 3.5 oz.	Once or twice a week instead of vegetables	Choline, vitamins, fiber
Rice	I00 cal per 2.5 oz.	Twice weekly—2.5 oz.	Carbohydrate
Pasta	I40 cal per 3.5 oz.	Once weekly	Carbohydrate
Egg	75 cal per egg	Once weekly—scrambled, no salt	Most nutrients, vitamins D, B6, biotin, iron
Oil supplements (fish, kelp, linseed)	According to type	According to size and need	Vitamin D, omega 3 and 6
Daily vitamin supplement	According to breed and size	According to size and need	To compensate for any deficiencies

CARING FOR YOUR PUPPY'S HEALTH

Daily Checks

Grooming—Grooming is essential, whatever the coat type. Through grooming, puppies learn to be touched on their different body parts while standing on a table or the floor. Brushing not only removes loose hair but also encourages acceptance of handling, which is especially important for veterinary treatment. You may also find lumps and bumps, detect fleas or ticks, or spot grass seeds between the toes before they cause trouble.

Left: Regular handling by all family members encourages bonding and a sense of trust.

Teeth cleaning—This must be done regularly. Chews and bones do not clean teeth adequately, although they do help. Dog toothpaste and brushes with instructions are available in most pet stores. Any deviation from clean teeth and healthy pink gums should be checked by the vet. Homeopathic remedies advised by the vet may help clean very dirty teeth and prevent the need for later corrective surgery.

Eye cleaning—For many dogs, debris tends to form at the corners of the eyes. Carefully remove it with a pet wipe and, if excessive, check for an eye infection. Continual runny eyes may indicate an infection, allergy, or dietary deficiency and may require veterinary treatment.

Summer and winter checks—Check between pads and toes for trapped grass seeds or impacted snow and ice after walks. At regular intervals, check the skin for seasonal parasites. Dogs spend more time outside in the summer, coming into contact with parasites, and they get muddy underneath after winter walks. The hardened muddy lumps can get trapped in the coat, causing pain in vulnerable parts of the body.

Handling experience—Regular handling encourages socialization. Your puppy's natural understanding and acceptance of this may vary from breed to breed or with age. If your puppy is encouraged to be handled while having a general veterinary exam, he learns to trust you and more readily accepts training, grooming, or other attention as he becomes an adult.

Weekly Checks

Cleaning ears—Floppy long ears are particularly prone to collecting dirt and wax. Sometimes dirty ears can smell unpleasant and, if painful, may cause

Above: **After a walk, check for mud that may be trapped under the tummy and between the pads of the feet.**

your puppy to be "off" or a little snappy. Regularly cleaning with ear wipes and plucking the fine hairs growing inside the ears helps maintain clean, problem-free ears.

Cutting nails—Dogs' nails, like humans', grow and need trimming. If you are uncomfortable trimming nails, your vet will do it. Suitable clippers, which are not difficult to use, are available, but take care if the nails are brittle or susceptible to breakage. Your puppy has two types of nails to clip: the toe nails and the dew-claws on the sides of the legs.

Right: **Checking for lumps and bumps around your puppy's tummy allows for early detection of serious problems.**

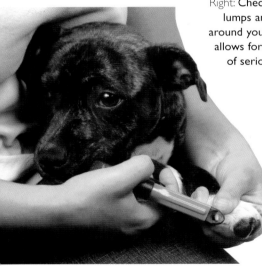

Above: **Use special clippers to cut your puppy's nails safely. Trimming the nails regularly helps prevent broken or sore nails.**

To cut nails: Pull the hair back from the nail, and identify where the quick (a pink tubelike center) is located inside the nail. This is where the nerve is located and must not be cut. Trim a little off the end of the nail, leaving approximately ¼ inch beyond the pink quick.

Monthly Checks

Keeping puppy clean—Bathe your dog about every four to six weeks to maintain the coat's condition. Some coat types benefit from bathing only once or twice a year to maintain the natural waterproof texture, so do consult the breeder. Regular brushing reduces dirt buildup.

Sex-related checks—Check the dog's testicles regularly for signs of lumps, and check around the nipples on bitches for lumps as well. This can be done during a bath or while grooming. Entire (not spayed) bitches can be prone to mammary tumors. These can be surgically removed to prevent the lumps from increasing or becoming malignant.

Urine/feces checks—Occasionally, observe the color, texture, and smell of your dog's urine and feces, as these can reveal early signs of health problems, even in a dog that appears to be healthy. Early treatment may prevent complications and expensive vet bills. Feces can be checked most easily when you poop-scoop to clean up after the dog. Loose bowel movements may mean that the dog has worms, or the cause may be dietary. An irritated bowel may produce a loose, mucus-covered, sometimes blood-stained stool; by the same token, a diet high in fat can cause very dry stools. Somewhere in between is about right.

Yearly Checks

Inoculations—A full course administered in early life is recommended. Opinion about vaccinations given later in life is divided regarding possible side effects, the necessary frequency, which to give, and the recommended requirements. Some owners and vets believe that the protection given by some vaccinations can be provided by homeopathy. If your puppy is boarded while you go on vacation, the boarding kennel will require certain vaccinations.

Above: **Yearly checks allow you to monitor your puppy's health and discuss any problems.**

Veterinary health checks—Most vets complete a full exam at the time of vaccinations, which involves listening to the heart, checking the mouth, examining the history of any injuries during the preceding year, and assessing general well-being. General advice on breed problems or infor-mation about maturity and the advisability of spaying or neutering can be discussed.

Lifetime Checks

These may be one-time checks given at a specific time of your puppy's life or very occasional checks that may be repeated. Discuss what is necessary with a knowledgeable breeder first. You should know which problems could arise in your breed and what tests are offered. Discuss these at the yearly visit to the vet. It is sensible to recognize any signs and symptoms of breed illnesses and inform the breeder of any problems. Some breed clubs or interested groups may, on request, provide a health checklist. The AKC and parent clubs take breed-specific problems seriously, conducting ongoing research and updating breeders and owners.

Hip X-ray—Because of the higher incidence of dislocated hips, usually experienced by medium to large breeds, recognized hip-check methods are available. When purchasing, you may have been shown hip scores, indicating that the sire and dam have good hip ratings and are therefore unlikely to pass hip dysplasia on to their progeny. If you plan to breed, your dog needs an X-ray evaluation on his hip joints done after he reaches two years of age. Other orthopedic problems should have been discussed and can also be checked using similar programs.

Hip X-rays can be taken at two years of age.

Above: **If your puppy is well socialized, he will not mind being checked by the vet.**

Checklist for X-rays

- No food or drink from 8:00 p.m. the night before.
- Allow the dog to relieve himself before the appointment.
- Take registration papers and pedigree for verification.
- Ensure that the dog is of an appropriate age for the test to be done.
- Arrive on time and arrange a time for picking him up.

Eye Testing—Some breeds suffer from inherited eye problems, and puppies may have been tested before purchase. Tests frequently require rechecking at a later date. In the United States, the main eye-testing registry is the Canine Eye Registration Foundation (CERF). CERF certifies dogs as free of hereditary eye disease through eye examinations by members of the American College of Veterinary Oph-

Above: **A well-handled dog is unlikely to object to having his eyes checked.**

thalmologists. The ophthalmologist completes a form that details the results of each eye exam, and dogs that are found to be clear of disease can be certified with CERF. CERF also maintains

databases based on all test results in order to identify disease patterns and aid in research.

Checklist for Eye Testing

- Find an accredited veterinarian in your area. Sometimes breed clubs or kennel clubs hold CERF testing in conjunction with shows or other events.
- Take treats to use as a reward for good behavior or as a distraction.
- If this is done at a show, ask to be tested after showing.

Blood Testing—Some breeds suffer health problems requiring blood tests. In some cases, blood tests can identify DNA markers, which signal predisposition to certain inherited illnesses. If you plan to breed your puppy, seek advice on the need for, accuracy of, and frequency of such tests.

Checklist for Blood Tests

- Ask for a copy of the test results.
- Follow any instructions about not feeding before testing.
- Request that a sample is kept for DNA storage if appropriate.

Miscellaneous Tests—Some breeds undergo various tests that may be revealed only when you purchase your puppy. This may be because the condition has not yet arisen throughout the entire breed, or it may be because the breeder is being cautious. Ask questions and find out what these involve before you purchase your puppy, and ask yourself if you are willing to undertake the necessary tests if you do purchase a puppy of that breed.

Internal and External

Roundworm—*Toxocara canis* worms pass to the puppy through the dam. Bitches are usually wormed before they whelp, but your puppy still needs to be treated in case he has ingested any when he suckled or licked his mother (who cleans up all his feces) or played outside in the garden. These eggs are not infectious at first, so it is important that any feces are cleaned up before they become infectious to humans, as infection by roundworms can cause blindness.

Tapeworms—*Dipylidium caninum* live in the small intestine of the host, and egg-bearing sections may, if expelled in the feces, be seen hanging on the hair around the anus if they are developing in sufficient quantities.

Hookworms and Whipworms—These live in the intestinal tract and ingest blood; they cause anaemia, diarrhea, or poor condition.

Heartworm—*Dirofilaria immitis* is caught from mosquitoes or fleas. These, as the name implies, live in the heart and require a yearly vaccine to rid the dog of them. If untreated, they can cause heart failure. Your vet will perform a heartworm test at your dog's annual check-up and then prescribe a monthly preventive, usually provided in tablet form.

You should bring a stool sample to your dog's annual vet visits so that it can be checked for certain internal parasites. Some worms, such as tapeworms, are visible to the eye, so you might notice them in your dog's stool. If so, contact your vet, who will ask you to bring in a stool sample. If worms are detected, your vet will prescribe an appropriate dewormer.

Fleas, Ticks, and Lice—Fleas, ticks, and lice may be found on your puppy if he likes to burrow into undergrowth that other animals inhabit, or if your puppy associates with other dogs, or if you have animals such as groundhogs in your yard. Fleas are the most common problem, and they stay in your puppy's coat long enough to complete their life cycle, during which they suck blood and lay eggs. The eggs do not stick to the coat but will fall off as your puppy moves around. It is not uncommon to have fleas living in soft furnishings, so if you have a heavy infestation, you may need to treat your home as well. There are a number of things you can do to stop this from becoming a problem, however. Ticks are dangerous, as they can transmit diseases when they attach to your dog. Lice are an itchy problem that can be treated by your veterinarian.

> **Expert Tip**
> Different flea and tick preventives contain different ingredients; some are not advised for all breeds. Discuss this with your vet.

Parasite Preventives

There are different preventives available for protecting your dog from certain internal parasites, fleas, and ticks. Your vet must prescribe the heartworm preventive, as your dog must first test free of heartworm; a dog infected with heartworm can be harmed by taking the preventive. Most heartworm preventives come in chewable tablet form, usually in flavors that dogs like, given once monthly; they also protect against several other worms. Flea and tick preventives are also typically given monthly. The most common type is a liquid that is applied to a small area of the dog's skin between the shoulder blades. The medicine spreads to kill any existing fleas and prevent new fleas and ticks from infesting your dog.

To reduce the incidence of fleas try:

- Flea collars—check the package for age and size guidelines.
- Flea preventives—available from the vet.

Infestation	Site	Effect	Evidence
Fleas	Lower back; above the tail; around the tummy; in the bed, carpet, and furnishings.	Intense itching, irritation caused by blood sucking, allergic reaction, flea bites on humans. One flea quickly increases to many fleas.	Small specks of grit in the coat; fleas seen moving around; if you place specks on a damp tissue, rings of blood form around them.
Mites	Different sorts can affect the skin all over the body.	Depending on the type, they can cause intense irritation, erupting skin condition, or flaky skin.	Severe dermatitis on the skin. There may be evidence of certain types visibly moving on the skin.
Ticks	Round bean-shaped lumps attached to the skin; can be grouped together in areas on the body.	Ticks suck the blood and can increase the incidence of certain diseases.	Larger tick hangs like a bean on the skin. Deer-tick bites have "bull's eye" appearance.

1

2

3

4

5

Flea larva (1). Adult flea (2). Ticks (3) can be felt under the coat. *Cheyletiella* mites (4) cause loose flakes of skin (5).

- Shampoo—usually medicated and purchased from the pet store.
- Homeopathic powders to use in the home on furniture and carpets.
- Tea-tree oil shampoo—can be used as a deterrent and purchased from the pet shop.
- Garlic tablets in the food—the author believes a daily dose in food helps with flea problems.

Veterinary advice may be needed because the itching can become severe if an allergy to fleas develops, caused by hypersensitivity to the flea saliva. The reaction experienced is so intense, the dog can scratch himself raw in a matter of hours.

ROUTINE GROOMING

Bathing does not have to be a chore, but at least half an hour needs to be set aside every four to six weeks during the summer months, and every six to eight weeks in the winter months for the average pet.

Regular grooming may reduce the number of occasions bathing is needed, but to keep the coat in tip-top condition, both are to be encouraged. Do not be put off by the vast array of shampoos and conditioners available. Ask the breeder for advice on what to use, and take this as a starting point before trying others. Always read the instructions; they often state an age at which use is suitable or indicate suitability for different coat types.

> **Some questions to ask when choosing a shampoo:**
>
> - Is there a type of shampoo that's best for my dog's breed?
> - Is my dog's age appropriate to the recommendation on the bottle?
> - Do I want to shampoo my dog for a special occasion, such as for showing?
> - Does my dog have a long coat, and, if so, which shampoo will be best for it?
> - Do I want my dog to smell clean or fresh and not "doggy?"
> - Would my dog's coat benefit from an odor-reducing type of shampoo?

Shampoo choices are varied, and the choice can be based on:

- Personal preference—the smell is pleasant.
- Insecticidal action—to deter fleas, mites, etc.
- Color shampoo—suitable for a specific coat color.
- Herbal shampoo—tea-tree oil or other herbal fragrance.
- Oil shampoo—such as mink oil or wheat germ oil, which can give the coat an extra shine.
- Puppy shampoo—for very young dogs.
- Breed shampoo—designed for specific coat types.
- Dry shampoo—useful for older dogs, particularly in winter.

Choosing Conditioners

Conditioner, like shampoo, needs to be considered in terms of coat type. Some coats will benefit from conditioning, and for those the choice may be whether to buy a combined shampoo and conditioner or to purchase each separately. Some coats may get dirty quicker if a conditioner is used.

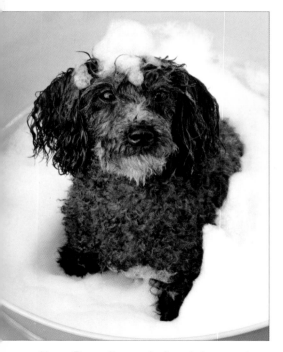

Above: **Depending on the breed, dogs require bathing every four to six weeks to maintain cleanliness and good coat condition.**

Giving the Bath

The procedure for this is not really that different from the way humans wash their own hair. For some of the smaller breeds, a specially sized plastic bath can be purchased. For medium or large breeds, long- or short-haired, a conventional bath with a shower attachment on the faucet can be used. The sequence is as follows:

- Prepare your bathroom with all items on hand: shampoo, towel, nail clippers, ear cleaner, and perhaps a treat in your pocket.

  - Fill the bath with a couple of inches of comfortably warm water (*left*).
  - Entice your puppy to come into the bathroom or carry him in.
  - Remove the collar and flea collar.
  - Place your puppy in the bath and use the shower spray to completely wet the coat with comfortably warm water.

- Use the appropriate amount of shampoo as stated on the bottle.
- Lather well and rinse with clean water, taking care to avoid the eyes (*below*).

> **Safety Tip**
> Do remember to kneel down beside the bath to avoid back strain!

- Shampoo a second time and rinse off very well. A shower spray or bucket will help.
- If a conditioner is used, rub it in and allow it to soak in for a minute or two before rinsing off. Make sure the coat is well rinsed after the bath.

- Towel dry (*right*) and leave your puppy to air dry in a warm room.
- Don't forget to provide clean bedding when your puppy is completely dry; use another dry towel to line the bed until then.
- Comb or brush the coat through when it is dry to remove any loose hairs, although long coats may benefit from being left for 24 hours to settle.

> **Expert Tips**
> - While the conditioner soaks in, you may like to use this opportunity to cut the nails or clean the ears with a proprietary cleaner provided by the vet for this purpose.
> - If your puppy has tar in his coat, soak the hair in vegetable oil, leave it to soak, then bathe. If this does not remove it, you may have to cut the soiled fur out of the coat.

Personal Grooming for Your Puppy

Grooming and trimming is a specialized activity. You may decide to trim your puppy yourself or take him to a groomer. Grooming is done on a regular basis to help with bonding, but it also socializes your puppy and helps him accept you as his leader. Dogs shed throughout the year, but more so at certain times than others.

With regular grooming, you brush out dead hair along with dirt trapped near the skin. Dead hair is trapped in the new growth and needs combing out, or it will mat and tangle. These mats can cause pain around major joints during movement or when you remove them with a comb. Even nonshedding breeds need brushing.

Short coats—Brush regularly with rubber, slicker, or bristle brushes to remove the shed hair, dirt, and dead skin. Work lengthwise along your puppy's body from front to back, following the lay of the hair. A damp chamois to finish adds luster to smooth coats. Wiry coats may need to be stripped, so consult the breeder to show you how to do this.

Medium-length coats—Brush daily, using a slicker brush or comb to remove the shed hair, dirt, and flakes of skin. Work along the lay of the coat, emptying the brush or comb of accumulated hair as necessary. Pay particular attention to the paws, the area around the anus, the ears, and the tail.

Long coats—An all-over groom is essential, as long coats collect dirt quickly. Use a slicker brush to remove the tangles, then comb down to the skin and draw out the dead hair. Mats and tangles can be removed with a dematting comb or gently teased out with a wide-tooth comb. Thinning scissors can be used to cut across tangles and release knots. A bristle brush adds sheen to silky coats, and sprays can be purchased to help remove tangles and condition very long coats. Always use the comb or brush along the lay of the coat, and try not to brush the coat in the opposite direction or dig the brush into the skin.

Keeping Your Puppy's Ears Clean

Most dogs grow fine ear hairs, which can become dirty and smelly. A dark wax builds up, and ear mites thrive in the warm, moist conditions. You can use a special ear powder, which dries the moist environment and prevents wax, but you also need a regimen of plucking the hair regularly.

Pluck out the fine fluffy hairs growing in the ear. If your puppy is long-haired, trim the external areas to allow air to ventilate the ear. Use ear wipes, recommended for cleaning

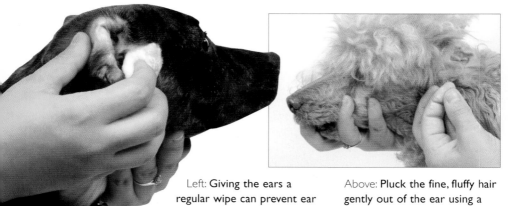

Left: **Giving the ears a regular wipe can prevent ear problems from developing.**

Above: **Pluck the fine, fluffy hair gently out of the ear using a finger and thumb.**

around the ear. If you notice signs of ear problems, take your puppy to the vet because these are painful. Ask your breeder what remedies are typically used for the breed to prevent further problems.

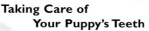

Taking Care of Your Puppy's Teeth

A total of 28 deciduous teeth erupt within the first few weeks of life, and these are shed at around 12 to 16 weeks of age (like human milk teeth), depending on the breed. By 7 months, most dogs have their 42 adult teeth.

Occasionally the deciduous teeth are retained, and surgery may be required to remove them to allow the permanent ones to erupt. This is important for a show puppy because the bite is part of the conformation. Most breeds have a scissors bite: the top teeth lie closely in front of the bottom. Some breeds have undershot bites (in which the teeth of the lower jaw project beyond the upper teeth) or overshot bites. Deviations from the bite expected for the breed will not usually cause problems, unless you plan to breed or show.

Above: **Hard bones are good to chew to help clean teeth, but brushing is still necessary.**

Proper dental care is essential, as bad or decaying teeth cause pain and disease. If severe gum infections occur, gums can bleed, and your puppy's breath will smell "doggy." Pockets of bacteria develop, and infections can get into the bloodstream and travel to the heart, liver, and kidneys. Tooth decay is caused by plaque (food, bacteria, and saliva) sticking to the teeth below the gum line. Periodontal disease develops when the plaque mineralizes and forms tartar, which is hard to remove once formed.

There are several chewing items, such as nylon bones with small bumps that act like dental floss when chewed, teeth-cleaning sticks, and so on. Feeding your puppy hard biscuits, bones, and chews helps considerably, but these cannot substitute for giving your puppy's teeth good regular cleanings. For advice on how to do this, see *The Puppy Handbook* pages 18–19.

Left and above left: **Clean, well-looked-after teeth will last your puppy for his lifetime.**

NATURAL DOG BEHAVIOR

Different breeds of dog exhibit different behaviors that are instinctive to them because humans specifically bred particular traits into dogs for specific purposes.

Some owners purchase a puppy for reasons such as "the breed is good with children," or "we thought they looked so nice and friendly," or "we met one on vacation, and he was so well behaved that we decided it was the breed for us." However, it pays to research the background of your breed, as many dogs end up being rehomed because the owner failed to understand them and could not train them.

Above: **Your puppy will use a play bow to entice you to give him attention or play a**

Below: **Barking expresses a need to show a feeling or emotion.**

Barking—Often a response to stimuli or to attract attention. This behavior can include a repertoire of howling, barking, whining, and growling. You may unwittingly use body language that causes your puppy to bark. Barking can become an action associated with the need to express a feeling or emotion such as "I'm lonely" or "There's someone there." Problems with barking relate to overattachment to the owner, fear, separation anxiety, boredom, insecurity, and attention seeking.

Canine body language—All mammals use body language as silent communication. Body posture, the way a dog walks, and the angle at which he holds his tail are important behavioral indicators of feelings. Try to understand what particular behaviors reveal about how your puppy is feeling. Observing your puppy will help you learn which behaviors indicate which emotions your dog is feeling: for example, happy tail wagging, a warning bark with tail stiff and straight up in the air, and a play bow with excited wagging motion to entice play or attract attention.

Chasing—Chasing is another form of hunting. Most puppies enjoy chasing around the yard, and it helps build confidence in their surroundings. Play between older dogs is sequenced into taking turns chasing each other. Dogs frequently try to chase birds or rabbits. This gets out of hand only if your puppy starts to feel territorial. Research shows that 2 percent of male dogs and 1 percent of bitches will chase people or cars.

Chewing—Chewing is normal and helps adult teeth erupt. It also alleviates boredom. Older dogs may enjoy chewing a large raw marrow bone, which stimulates a natural activity, helps

Right: **Chewing is a normal behavior that encourages teeth to erupt.**

keep teeth strong, and removes plaque. Hard nylon bones or other chew toys are usually enjoyed. Dogs love rawhide, but it should be offered only under supervision.

Above: **Certain dogs dig a lot because this is natural behavior for them.**

Digging—Some breeds (terriers especially) dig more than others because they were bred to hunt to ground. Dogs dig to bury bones or toys, to make dens to whelp puppies, or to make a hole. Some dogs dig for no reason, apparently for pleasure or to follow a scent.

Hunting and stalking—Hunting and stalking are practice for developing survival skills. This innate need to track the scent of rabbits or other animals may be in certain breeds and not others. Different breeds can "turn off" this process at particular developmental stages. Hunting and stalking behaviors can involve anything from playing to holding objects in the mouth to stalking and heading off the "prey" to holding and "immobilizing" toys.

Guarding food—Guarding objects, particularly food, is not uncommon. You may be upset when your puppy guards his food bowl or a place in his crate where he has hidden food. This causes a

Safety Tip
Do not let your puppy chew shoelaces, as they can be swallowed.

problem only if it is allowed to get out of hand, as aggression can develop. Training very early on to accept your commands is essential.

Retrieving—Some dogs enjoy holding objects in their mouths. It is part of the genetic makeup of some breeds to carry items carefully without causing damage. Gundogs in particular have soft mouths and will carry game without damaging it.

Running—The "genes" for running and for body shape are synonymous. Certain breeds were bred for running and thus have a lean powerful shape, optimal for running at speed.

Scenting and tracking—Smell is the first experience of life and is crucial to survival. When a dog goes for a walk, he sniffs fences or posts to see who has passed by. Dogs sniff the ground or the air, according to how their genetic makeup tells them to retrieve and store information. Social greetings occur by mutual sniffing of the mouth and genitals because this identifies specific odors that signify status. Dogs sniff their owners when the owners return home; it tells them whether they have eaten and what contacts have been made. Male dogs will become aroused if they smell a bitch in season.

Shaking—Puppies enjoy shaking toys. This is related to the killing instinct. Growling, worrying the item, and shaking the life out of it allows the pup to engage in instinctive behavior. Other puppies will join in the fun, and a tug of war sometimes breaks out with everyone trying to gain possession of the toy.

Building on Your Puppy's Natural Behaviors

Your puppy will be good at learning, memorizing, and problem solving, and he will learn to adapt to your home environment. He needs a bit of all of these skills to survive, and one skill will be better developed than the others.

Your puppy will be constantly exploring his environment through play, taking in stimuli via his senses of smell, sight, and sound. This environ-

Safety Tips
- Make sure that all visitors to your home follow the same basic rules regarding behavior that you want your puppy to observe right from the start.
- Put your puppy in a suitable place out of the way when children or elderly people are visiting if he becomes overly excited, and let him out only when he is calm and behaving well.

Above: **Dogs constantly "read" the environment when out and about by sniffing everything with which they come into contact.**

mental interaction and contact with you will have a profound effect on his life experiences and social responses, so many natural behaviors can be used for your training purposes.

Your puppy adapts his natural behaviors to fit in with your life by making them part of his domestic routine. An example of this is training through play. Retrieving breeds can be taught games that allow them to use their skill by harnessing their natural instinct to understand what you are teaching them. This has also been useful in training

assistance dogs, which use their natural abilities to retrieve items for their disabled owners, alert them to visitors at the door, or indicate that the phone is ringing. The mental stimulation of taking part in interesting activities helps develop your puppy's skills and prevents boredom. If he's bored, your puppy will just find something else to occupy his mind!

Reward Only Good Behavior

To fit into your lifestyle, your puppy needs socialization at a time when the best window of opportunity is presented. You must teach him the right way to fit in with your family. Activities seen as natural behavior are often viewed with pride by owners because they are pleased to have a puppy that can move in a particular way, catch toys, or perform tricks. However, your puppy may also have learned that instead of fighting to gain dominance and get his own way, he can shape and *train you* to provide for him without showing aggression! These days the technique of rewarding only good behavior and distracting or ignoring bad behavior is being used to solve problem behaviors.

Left: **Use games to encourage your puppy to develop his natural behaviors.**

Problems Associated with Natural Behaviors

Problem	Natural behavior	Solution
Over-excitement	This is the level of arousal that develops when dogs in the wild kill prey; the behavior involves predatory aggression to be first in the line for food.	Never allow overexcitement when playing, which could cause bad behavior. Stop the activity to teach your puppy that this behavior spoils the fun.
Playing too roughly	Predatory behavior is developed through play in the litter and is a precursor to learning how to socialize with their siblings or their mother.	Prevent roughness by immediately stopping playtime and then ignoring your puppy. He will associate this with similar behavior learned from his mother.
Biting	Puppies learn from biting during play the degree of force that they can apply. If the bite is too hard and stops the game, a puppy learns to recognize the amount of force that will stop his fun.	When the puppy bites too hard, ignore him or stop playing. This will teach him to play nicely. This is what his siblings and mother would have done.
Attention seeking	This can stem from a dominant dog feeling that he has a higher status in the "pack" and demanding to receive attention when he feels he should have it.	Develop a routine when your puppy knows he will get attention, but he should also learn that there are times when his owner is not able to play.
Dominance	In litters, one puppy may dominate submissive puppies and direct the way games are played.	Play regularly, but make sure your puppy wins tugs and tussles only occasionally.
Problems with toys	During the kill, wild animals will rip the prey to pieces to obtain their own share or the best portion.	Give indestructible toys. These provide interest and allow puppies to explore objects in acceptable ways.
Possession	Food is important when competing with rivals, and maintaining control over possessions is necessary to survival. Possession signifies the prize of the hunt.	Establish which toys are for playing with you and which are for when your puppy has to amuse himself. "Swap" the toy for a treat when you want it back.
Boredom	In the wild, dogs would simply find something else to do, with no one to direct their behavior.	Dogs need stimulation to learn. They will find something else to play with (or destroy) if left alone with no stimulus.

SOCIALIZATION

Between 5 and 18 weeks is the best time for socializing a puppy. Puppies develop through learning but need to experience changes within their comfort zone and learn how to problem solve.

Puppies' nervous systems and senses are immature and cannot react appropriately to, or remember, previous experiences until five weeks of age, when human contact reinforces early social skills by repeating them frequently and rewarding good behavior.

At five weeks, your puppy's brain is close to being of adult proportions and capable of learning acquired skills. Puppies constantly need more activities and stimuli; some to develop an ability to cope with frustration and others to learn how to cope with more complex challenges. Research shows that puppies subjected to very mild stress, such as that caused by seeing different environments or hearing new noises, actually benefit at this age. Any new experiences must be positive so your puppy can learn to understand a variety of different situations and how to deal with difficulties that may crop up later.

Socializing from Eight to Twelve Weeks

Assuming the breeder has familiarized the litter with everyday sounds around the house, the

Above: **Introduce your puppy to other family pets as soon as possible. Teach him that dominant behavior is unacceptable.**

repertoire of noises your puppy can cope with when you bring him home should be quite large. Your puppy will have some idea of his personal space in relation to his toys, where to toilet, and where to eat. Outside experiences may have included traveling in the car and visiting the vet. Continually providing new stimuli is essential at this time, and there are many ways this can be achieved while your puppy becomes familiar with you. He cannot go out or meet other dogs until his immunization program is complete, so early socializing must take place in your home. See *The Puppy Handbook* pages 22–25 for further ideas.

Twelve Weeks to Six Months

This is the most important time to practice the lessons learned in the outside world. Basic training should be consistent when out taking walks, meeting people and other dogs, exploring new things, and learning through play. You need to show your puppy lots of new places where he can sniff and explore, and

Socialization skills can be learned at a young age.

Left: **Early socialization with other dogs and animals is important for compatibility with other species.**

Above: **Introduce your puppy to family members, friends, and neighbors within a few days of arriving at his new home.**

introduce new objects to investigate. If your puppy has grown to respect and trust you, he will feel confident and happy in your presence when he meets new people, dogs, or unfamiliar objects.

Noises—Once settled in your home, there will be other strange noises your puppy needs to hear and become familiar with. Soothe your puppy by stroking him gently or holding him in your arms if he is frightened, but do not go closer to the noise until the puppy appears happy for this to happen. If your puppy is distressed, move away from the noise and try again another time. Introduce the noise later, gradually bringing your puppy closer until he seems at ease with what is going on.

People—Introduce your puppy to neighbors, family, and friends soon after he has come home, but not right away. Discourage your puppy from jumping up on people, and teach him to come when called.

Other household pets—Older dogs must not be made to feel jealous and must be allowed to establish their position as top dog, with your puppy at the bottom of the pecking order. Take particular care with cats, which may scratch, and horses, which may kick if the puppy barks and runs around their feet.

Your home environment—Familiarization should start immediately within the first week at home so acceptable boundaries are established.

Some good examples are:

- If your puppy is not allowed upstairs, block off the stairs or make sure he does not learn to climb the stairs (*right*) and, if he attempts to do so, bring him back downstairs where he belongs.
- If he is not allowed in the flower bed in the yard, keep him out of it at all times.
- If your puppy is house-trained and has already learned to do his business outside, show him where you want his toileting area to be.
- Teach your puppy where he will sleep, eat, and spend the main part of every day.
- Teach him where he will stay when you have to go out.
- Make sure your puppy is secure in the yard with the gate closed so he cannot go out into the street.

Above: **A secure gate and high fencing around the yard will keep your puppy safe.**

THE IMPORTANCE OF PLAY

Play and stimulation are essential throughout your puppy's early life, but play remains a natural activity for all dogs from birth to old age. Play starts at about two and a half weeks old, as soon as puppies open their eyes and recognize their companions.

Right: **Stalking or pouncing on toys is a natural behavior stemming from the hunting instinct your puppy is born with.**

In the early days, play offers a means for learning how to interact and develop the skills a puppy will need for survival. As puppies become active and interact with each other, they will start to develop a repertoire of skills according to the nature of their instinctive behavior.

Above: **Puppies must learn the consequences of biting your fingers.**

Many of these early play activities relate to establishing a hierarchy within the family group. Through the social rules of a family network, a bond forms across different generations within a group. Younger dogs instinctively learn about touch and sensitivity through playing with adult dogs. If puppies are too rough and fight or bite too hard, their elders will either reprimand them or withdraw their attention. By acting out certain behaviors in a ritualistic manner, such as biting each other, puppies can learn bite inhibition—meaning how hard they can bite in play and how hard to bite if conflict occurs.

Managing Problem Behaviors

Some problem behaviors may occur as a result of early removal from the litter, which prevents puppies from learning social skills at the right age. However, if good play behavior is encouraged, your puppy will quickly learn how to behave appropriately toward you. Establishing social behavior is an excellent way for your puppy to learn how to interact with you, and using playtime as a reward after training reinforces his bond with you. Playtime can be withheld as a way of withdrawing your attention and to call a "time out" if your puppy becomes overexcited or is biting too hard. Timing is crucial, and this sanction should not be overused. Employ it only when your puppy can make the direct association between the problem behavior and your withdrawal of attention.

If you watch your puppy playing, you will see that puppy activities belong to recognizable natural adult behavior. For example, when your puppy stalks and pounces on a toy, it is evidence that your puppy is born already programmed with natural hunting behavior. Learning to discriminate what are and what are not appropriate objects to stalk and pounce on is a specific biological use of play. Games and toys can develop this natural approach, although you want to discourage any aggressive behavior.

Game Playing

Your puppy will try to invite you to play using body language, so you will be able to predict when your puppy wants to play. From early on, puppies learn to attract attention by pulling, nipping, chasing, and retrieving toys or objects. These actions also help them learn how to interact and can develop and stimulate their minds. Using these behaviors in a game teaches your puppy how to interact with his immediate environment and can be used to provide an early start in training. Game playing is a great stimulus for dogs, who often spend part of each day alone. Toys filled with treats (*below*) can be given to a dog as you leave the house; these toys stimulate a natural ability to seek out the treat by problem-solving and also encourage the dog to persevere to reach the reward.

Stimulating Natural Intelligence

Through play, your puppy will reinforce, in the context of a game, many of the natural instincts that dogs still use in certain situations. Encourage your puppy to play frequently during the early socialization period because he will grow up to be more intelligent and more able to problem solve in different situations. Scientists who have studied the brains of dogs suggest that if a dog's development is enriched with good socializing and stimulation, his brain will be larger and have more neural connections than the brains of dogs that develop in impoverished conditions. Puppies that miss out on early learning can be deprived of a range of social skills and may become fearful as a result. Playing too

Safety Tip
Put all your puppy's toys away when they are not needed to avoid anyone falling or tripping on them.

aggressively with more dominant puppies can also teach the puppy incorrect behavior patterns, making him more difficult to train in the future.

Toys can be purchased in abundance in pet stores, but finding the right type of toy for an individual dog is important. For example, toys intended to be shaken may be more appropriate for breeds that naturally shake their prey to kill it. Dogs that enjoy problem solving may get greater enjoyment from toys that need to be "figured out" to reap the rewards. So it is important to appreciate that toys and games can be chosen for breed-specific reasons.

Games also help young muscles grow stronger.

Left: **A dog that is given plenty of stimulation will develop a quick and active brain.**

Understanding Your Puppy's Playfulness

Play involves movement, communication, thought, and creativity. It gives pleasure and can be enjoyed alone, in pairs, or in a group. Play reinforces your puppy's natural instincts.

Dogs equipped to survive indulge in specific play activities, and through those activities they can practice skills that allow them to problem solve when changes occur in their environment. Play in your adult dog will also be a way of communicating with you. Your puppy will draw on his natural behavior to start to play when he meets other dogs and also to communicate the desire to play with you. This means of communication is instinctive but, more interestingly, is also universal.

Above: **Play in very young puppies is often a cycle of dominance and submission.**

The communication of the desire to play can encompass various types of behavior:

Facial expression—In play, this is often revealed by a relaxed mood, with soft eyes looking intently but not staring. Your puppy's ears will be forward or flopped, his mouth open with the lips showing some teeth and giving the impression of smiling. Some dogs give a grin by folding back the upper lip or by leaving the tongue hanging out.

Body posture—Your puppy will hold his head in a normal midway position and may invite you to play using a play bow. In this position, the head and chest are low and the rump is elevated. Your puppy encourages more play with other dogs by successive shows of submission or dominance, either placing the front paws on the other's back at the shoulder or rolling over. His tail position is likely to be alert, confident, and wagging excitedly.

Vocalizing—You may hear your puppy whining excitedly and giving an occasional bark when he anticipates a play session. Barking is one of the most common dog noises and is a natural behavior. It signals to another dog (or you) that your puppy wants to play or is saying hello, or it is a means of getting attention. The bark for "come-and-play-with-me" is a friendly woof with a noticeable touch of excitement and anticipation.

Movement and activity—The chase is a natural behavior adopted from previous generations, when dogs used to hunt and give chase.

Left: **Your puppy will appear to smile at you when he is in a relaxed mood.**

Above: **Chasing and tugging are natural instincts left over from the days of hunting for food.**

This chase is now a form of enticement to encourage another dog to play. You may notice that a dog that loves the chase way of playing will tear around at breakneck speed as if in a glorious game of tag. It's a game to see which dog can run the fastest or keep going the longest.

Using Play in Training and Learning

Early training, when your puppy is learning to live with you, can involve endless hours of fun in play. Once puppies are settled, they quickly learn the fun of coming when called when a reward is offered. Use play to train your puppy with a sequence of responses and rewards. You should act with gentleness and firmness (giving praise for good behavior) in ways your puppy finds stimulating. Don't practice for too long, or your puppy will tire or get bored. Puppies have short attention spans.

As many of your puppy's innate survival skills and natural behaviors are built on a process of response and reward, it should not take long for your puppy to learn other skills in the same way. This principle also applies to how you deal with any fears and wariness your puppy may exhibit as he grows up and can be used to support a program of desensitization to experiences that may frighten the dog. Your puppy learns to develop his skills through association with stimulus response exercises and so learns what behavior is acceptable to you. If these skills are learned through play, your puppy is more likely to make

the association that you are a source of affection and rewards if he continues to behave in a specific way. This bond between you and your puppy will strengthen throughout your training sessions as your puppy gets older and learns more.

Above: **Play can be a natural basis for introducing formal training.**

Stimulus response training is a method of learning that develops through the use of a reward—edible or emotional (e.g., petting)—or it can be learned through the use of lure and reward training or clicker training. In each case, play can be used as the basis for formal training, although your puppy will be unaware of the connection. He will view the experience just as a playful task that he enjoys achieving and for which he gets rewarded. In this way, good behavior can be learned through play and socialization, developing the bond you have established.

PUPPY TRAINING

Your puppy will be trained by using four specific aspects of his life. These aspects are his physical well-being, his emotional state, his mental capacity or intelligence, and his social being.

Left: **Encourage your puppy to behave in acceptable ways.**

For these four areas to develop satisfactorily, your puppy needs to be introduced to different places, to be socialized to different people and other animals, and to learn by association with different events in his life how to respond in a particular way to a particular situation. A certain amount of his knowledge (around 40 percent) will be the result of heredity; the rest will be derived from his life experiences.

The basis of learning through training is the technique of practicing particular behaviors that reinforce actions you wish to encourage in certain circumstances. Your puppy learns to behave in a particular way because it results in rewarding consequences; he learns the cause-and-effect relationship between the cues you give and the response you want. Your puppy will repeat the acceptable behavior and consequently learn to succeed because you reward his correct response. In time, he also makes the association between not performing the expected behavior and not receiving a reward. This is called *operant conditioning*.

If a stimulus is given, usually a food treat, and your puppy responds as you want—so you achieve your aim of training a particular behavior—this is called *primary* or *positive* reinforcement. When paired with primary reinforcement for long enough, a learned response can eventually be elicited by a different reward. It does not necessarily need to be a food stimulus; it could be a toy, petting, or spoken words of praise such as "Good boy." This is called a *conditioned* reinforcement.

For early training, certain socializing methods (using primary reinforcement) are very suitable for preventing bad habits from being formed. However, more formal training methods, such as lure and reward or clicker training (using a conditioned reinforcement) will be necessary to develop greater skills for imprinting more advanced behavior.

Early Problem Solving Through Socializing

Play biting—Puppies learn from playing with littermates that play biting will cause a reaction if they bite hard enough, and in time they usually

Above: **Play biting teaches the puppy what reaction will occur if he bites too hard.**

learn how hard is acceptable. However, when puppies leave the litter, they may not have the "checks and balances" to keep this behavior under control. Deal with a play-biting problem immediately, as soon as it starts, or it could get out of hand. Say "No" loudly when it happens and ignore the puppy so he stops the play biting. Do not resume playing until the puppy realizes that the bite hurt you. Note: Do not pull your hand away too quickly, as the puppy's sharp little teeth can easily rip skin.

Left: **Teaching your puppy to take food gently from your hands and not to grab is important, particularly if you have children.**

Stealing food—Teaching your puppy to take food gently can be very useful. A recommended method is to hold a small treat next to his mouth while quietly saying "No." Wait momentarily, then pop the food into his mouth. If he has not grabbed it (which is unlikely if this training is started early), he should be congratulated and petted, and the sequence repeated. Teaching and practicing with other members of your family should work well to reduce food grabbing and play biting.

Fear aggression—This usually manifests itself in puppies that are insufficiently socialized or nervous in their new environments. Establish what caused the fear, and desensitize your puppy in small, easy stages. Take the dog toward the object or people who caused the reaction and hold him on the leash at a distance, without him becoming frightened. When he relaxes and does not appear so anxious, take him closer until he again seems to relax. Keep repeating this exercise until the puppy is close and no longer fearful or aggressive.

Separation anxiety—Every litter of puppies should become accustomed to being left on their own for short periods without human companions. A single puppy in a new home, however, may have to get used to a period of solitude quite quickly, and you are advised to build this up in small increments. Leaving a selection of toys for the puppy to play with and slowly increasing the time that you are away will help build trust and the understanding

Above: **All puppies need to learn how to stay on their own and behave themselves without getting upset or overly anxious.**

that you will return. If your puppy shows signs of distress, go back to shorter time periods and slowly increase the duration. If the distress persists, consult a vet.

Clicker Training Your Puppy

Clicker training focuses on using operant conditioning to teach your puppy a desired behavior and to perform a correct response for a positive reinforcement or no reward.

Your puppy will learn faster if a conditioned response for using the clicker is established first by offering a reward. Pairing the clicker (the conditioned reinforcement) with a reward (the primary reinforcement) communicates to your puppy the exact moment at which the correct behavior was delivered. If your timing is correct when you click and say "Good dog," your puppy cannot be confused about which behavior you're *marking*. A further advantage of the clicker is that its tone does not vary, so it delivers the same sound each time.

Initially, your puppy learns simply to associate the clicking noise with the reward of a treat. Later, after he's learned the response, you can use the clicker to reward behavior, and your puppy learns to anticipate a reward each time he performs correctly. Soon the sound of the clicker serves as a reward in itself, and you can extend the time between the click and the treat. This should continue until your puppy reacts correctly each time, pricking up his ears at the sound of the click. When your puppy behaves in a desired way, click each time until he realizes what you're clicking for. For example, a dog that jumps up may then drop to the ground on all fours; the owner then clicks, and the dog waits for and gets his reward, thus reinforcing the desired behavior of not jumping up.

To sum up the benefits of clicker training:

- More accurate than verbal praise and encourages your puppy to focus on you.
- Your puppy learns the behaviors you want by operant conditioning, through the process of reward (positive reinforcement) and non-reward.
- Clicker training allows communication across the barriers of language.
- Attracts your puppy and prevents distraction away from you.
- Removes food from the immediate picture, as your puppy is listening for the click at the moment of achievement.
- Your puppy learns to problem solve and learns from his actions what it is you are trying to get him to achieve.

Clicker training can be used in conjunction with luring. Using a treat to lure your puppy into a specific position, you click the clicker precisely at the moment

Left: **Use clicker training to teach your puppy specific behaviors.**

2

3

Above: **Use a treat to lure your puppy into a stand or a sit. A belly rub is a further reward for a job well done.**

of success and then reward him. By repeating this several times, your puppy learns by the timing of the click what behavior he was doing that earned the click. Your puppy ultimately learns the required behavior. By repeating this over and over in training, with the later introduction of your voice command, your puppy can learn any number of commands.

Using Lure and Reward Training

In this technique, a food treat (the reinforcement) is held close to your puppy's nose. The treat stimulates a response, and your puppy is lured into a position, such as a sit, and given the treat once correctly positioned. Your puppy makes an association between the position and the reward, which shapes the movement you want.

Your puppy can be lured into other positions because you withhold the treat until the movement is accomplished. As different commands are learned, you can string more than one command together to teach a sequence. For example, you can teach the dog to go down from a sit or to turn around. A crucial element in this process is that you reward your puppy for each piece of the sequence to encourage him to repeat the same movement

another time. Ultimately, once each individual command is mastered, only the complete sequence should be rewarded.

The lure and reward method of training depends on your puppy's well-developed sense of smell. A variety of strong-smelling treats should be used to keep your puppy's attention throughout training. Research shows dogs learn much faster and more successfully if they are allowed to participate voluntarily in this form of learning. It is important, however, that the reward is combined with visual or verbal cues so your puppy learns through your body language and tone of voice to establish communication with you. The psychological benefit of training includes the bonding relationship between you both, and therefore it provides a good foundation on which to build your relationship and sense of companionship.

Alternate the treat with a toy for variety and anticipation.

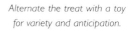

NEUTERING A PUPPY

The surgical removal of the canine reproductive parts is referred to as neutering for male dogs and spaying for female dogs. In the modern world, people have found it necessary to have their dogs sexually altered for a variety of reasons.

However, it is worth considering certain factors that might influence your decision.

- If done to combat behavioral problems, altering your puppy will not make him or her behave properly unless a new training regimen is planned at the same time.
- Obviously, a dog or bitch must be sexually intact if you plan to breed.
- A neutered or spayed dog cannot compete in AKC conformation shows. This makes sense, as dog shows are intended to select dogs worthy of breeding.

Neutering a Male Dog

Male dogs may be neutered for health reasons as advised by the veterinarian or for other reasons; many feel that it is the responsible choice for pet owners to have their dogs neutered so as not to contribute to the pet overpopulation problem that causes so many dogs to end up homeless. Neutering is usually same-day surgery. Male dogs have their testes surgically removed (*above left*), along with the scrotal sac, which removes the cells producing the hormone testosterone. A general anesthetic is required, and around ten stitches are inserted to hold the wound together until healing is complete. Your puppy may feel unwell for a few days, but he will recover quickly.

Disadvantages of Male Castration

Certain disadvantages have been reported, but the incidences are rare and all can be addressed by being vigilant and seeking medical advice if necessary.

Weight gain—Monitor your puppy's weight carefully after surgery, and if necessary cut back on your puppy's food slightly and increase the length of his daily walks.

Coat changes—Your puppy may have a poor coat condition after an anesthetic. Adding supplements and oils to the food may be necessary to rejuvenate the dog's coat after surgery.

Incontinence—There may be an underlying problem; take your puppy back to the vet.

Problems of Having a Bitch in Season

During estrus, which generally occurs about every six months, your bitch leaks blood and must learn to keep clean, or drops of blood will find their way onto carpets and furniture. The problem may occur when she has been sleeping and stands up to move around. If the bitch remains entire, encourage your puppy to clean herself by gently patting the inside leg when she lies down until she noses your hand. Reward her for cleaning herself. You can also buy special panties with liners to absorb the blood.

If you do not plan to breed or show, your vet will likely recommend having your female spayed for the health benefits and to eliminate the risk of unwanted litters.

Spaying a Bitch

It is generally agreed that the best time to spay a female for maximum health benefits is before the first heat cycle. Discuss this with your vet to get his opinion. Spaying involves the surgical removal of the uterus and ovaries under a general anesthetic. An incision is made in the

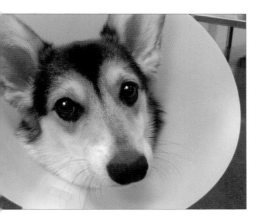

Above: **Post-operative care may necessitate a cone collar to prevent licking the wound.**

bitch's abdomen, requiring stitches, which are removed after ten days. Surgery is more invasive than for castration, and painkillers are needed post-operatively for up to 48 hours. Take care to prevent any licking or biting of the wound, and initially (following your vet's advice) allow only gentle exercise.

Reasons for Spaying Bitches

Unwanted puppies—Spayed bitches will obviously not be in a position to populate the world with unwanted puppies.

Inconveniences of estrus—Some owners find these cycles messy and inconvenient. Also, in multidog households with dogs of both sexes, the onset of estrus can lead to fighting.

Inconvenience of male interest—Some owners may find it extremely annoying to have male dogs hanging around the doorstep or following them home every time their bitch is in season.

Health benefits—Spaying greatly reduces the risk of mammary cancer and eliminates the possibility of uterine infections, as the uterus is removed.

Above: **Bitches in season may encourage the unwanted attentions of nearby male dogs.**

Disadvantages of Spaying

The disadvantages are similar to those listed for male dogs: weight increase, slight incontinence, and coat changes. However, most bitches only rarely, if ever, experience these.

Left: **Having puppies may be appealing, but it also imposes the responsibility of finding good homes for the puppies with suitable owners.**

HEALTH MATTERS

Puppies need vaccinating before going out into the world. Some immunity will be passed on from their mother's milk if her vaccinations are current, but this should not be relied on.

Your puppy will probably have his first shots between six and eight weeks of age, but some vets differ in their regimens.

First Aid and Your Puppy

Accidents can happen any time while you are out and about, and obviously you need to deal with them promptly based on what the problem is and what is available to you.

It is always useful to keep a first aid kit for your puppy in the car or at home. However, many items are probably already in your medicine cabinet, other than those that are purchased specifically for canine use.

Sprains and strains—Your puppy may limp painfully if he suffers a sprain or strain initially, but if there is no obvious difficulty with deformity, passive movement (when you mobilize the joint by hand), or severe pain, rest your puppy for a few

Dog Vaccination

Condition	Description	Immunization procedure
Leptospirosis	Gastroenteritis, increased thirst, high fever, low temperature, vomiting, kidney and liver problems later if the dog survives.	Usually given in combination shot (DHLPP) every 3 to 4 weeks between 6 and 16 weeks old. Yearly booster.
Canine distemper	Runny eyes, diarrhea, nasal discharge and a cough, seizures, and hard pads.	Same as above.
Infectious canine hepatitis	Highly contagious, fatal within 24 hours, affects the eyes and causes liver and kidney damage.	Same as above.
Parvovirus	Heart problems and pneumonia, vomiting, gastroenteritis.	Same as above.
Kennel cough or infectious tracheo-bronchitis	Two sorts, both highly contagious, causing severe cough as well as other respiratory symptoms.	Vaccination given as injection or nasal spray. Boostered every six months to one year.
Parainfluenza	Contagious respiratory infection.	Usually given in combination shot (DHLPP) every 3 to 4 weeks between 6 and 16 weeks old. Yearly booster.
Rabies	Nervousness, agitation, paralysis, "mad" behavior.	First shot given at four to five months old. Repeated in one year, then every one to three years, depending on vaccine used and local law.

days. If the problem does not improve, take your puppy to the vet.

Broken bones—These will need urgent veterinary care. The bone may appear to grind or be obviously out of place, so handle your puppy very carefully, with as little stress or movement as possible. Splint or hold the limb in place to immobilize it as much as possible.

Bleeding—Certain parts of the anatomy bleed more than others. The site of the bleeding will determine what needs to be done.

Internal bleeding: Check whether your puppy has something trapped in his mouth if blood appears on the teeth, gums, or tongue. If the blood is not coming from the gums or a cut, call the vet.

If the blood is from the anus, consider whether your puppy might have eaten something he should not have, in which case his stools may be mucus filled and bloody. If your puppy is otherwise active and well, withhold food but offer water, and reintroduce food after 24 hours with chicken and rice. See your vet immediately if blood loss is more than just a little, if it increases in volume, or if you have any cause for concern.

External bleeding: All serious wounds need prompt veterinary care. However, first aid may be needed to stem the flow of blood at the time of injury. Certain body parts, such as the ears, pads, and mouth, tend to bleed more profusely. If your puppy allows it, mop up the blood with clean tissues and examine the injury. If the wound is caused, for example, by a dog bite, apply gentle pressure with tissues or a dressing until the bleeding stops. Clean the wound with a suitable disinfectant, and apply a little antiseptic cream. For anything more substantial, try to stop the bleeding

Above: **Ear injuries bleed profusely, but first clean the wound, as it may be quite insignificant.**

> **Safety Tip**
> Avoid any contact with unknown or unvaccinated dogs until after your puppy's vaccinations are complete.

as best you can, and take your puppy straight to the vet. It is surprising, though, how a small wound can appear quite big until you clean up the blood and see what you are dealing with, so don't panic.

Wasp stings—Your puppy may be inquisitive about wasps because of the way they buzz! If the sting is in the mouth, check to see if there is a problem such as a swollen tongue or respiratory distress, and seek veterinary advice if you need to. If the sting is on the body, apply a little tea-tree oil or vinegar to neutralize the alkalinity of the venom and soothe the area.

Bee stings—Treat these like wasp stings with a little tea-tree oil, or apply a paste of baking soda and water. This is reputed to neutralize the acidity.

Snake bite—Although bites are uncommon, your response depends on the type of snake and your dog's age. Try to identify the type of snake and get to the vet as quickly as possible. Always check to see what exactly your dog is nosing around at.

Broken and bleeding nail or accidental nail trimming injury— If your puppy's nail breaks or you trim it a little too short, use a styptic pencil or powder to stop the blood flow. If you do not have either on hand, stem the flow with pressure over the end of the nail with your finger, and then soak the nail in a little salty water or disinfectant to prevent infection.

55

DAYS OUT WITH YOUR PUPPY

You may prefer to take your puppy with you when you go out for the day or on vacation. The alternative is to leave him in the care of a friend or neighbor or to arrange a boarding kennel or a dog sitter for longer visits. If you do choose to leave your puppy at home, you must give some thought as to what will happen in your absence.

Leaving Your Puppy at Home

Consider the following if your dog is staying at home and receiving outside care:

- Your dog sitter must be committed to your puppy's welfare.
- Make sure you leave full details of where you are going, including contact numbers, an emergency contact, and the vet's name, address, and phone numbers.
- Leave details of any medications or treatments necessary.
- Make sure the dog sitter knows how far and where to walk your dog.
- Provide outdoor leashes, a collar with an ID tag, poop bags, and coats (if used).
- If your dog has access to a yard, make sure that the gate is locked.
- Confirm what arrangements you would like if your puppy is involved in a fight, becomes ill, or comes into season.
- Make sure there is fresh water and regular social contact available during the day.
- Leave a detailed list for meals, explaining exact requirements.

Traveling with Your Puppy

- Give a small, light meal about two hours before traveling.
- Allow your puppy plenty of time to relieve himself before leaving home.
- If your puppy will be crated in the car, allow several weeks of practice so he is used to it

Above: **Securing your puppy on the back seat with a harness ensures his safety in the car.**

before departure day.

- Secure your puppy with a dog seat belt, in a crate, or behind a dog guard.
- Make sure the crate is well ventilated and large enough for your puppy to turn around comfortably.
- Provide frequent breaks to stop so your puppy can relieve himself and have a drink.
- Your puppy must have a strong leash and collar with an ID tag.

Camping and Hiking

Most brochures for vacation sites tell whether they are dog friendly, whether there is a charge for animals, and whether there is a designated area for families with dogs.

Above: **Secure your puppy close to your campsite, and do not let him wander around.**

Right: **Most dogs love to play on the beach on vacation, but do remember to rinse out the salt residue and sand afterward. Use shampoo and conditioner if necessary.**

Some general rules that should be observed:

- Keep your puppy on a collar and leash at all times.
- Clean up after your puppy.
- Ensure that your puppy behaves himself.
- Ensure that your puppy does not make excessive noise by barking.
- Ensure that your puppy is not left unattended in a camper or tethered in a tent.
- It is not permissible to take your puppy into the restrooms or to make use of the showers to clean your puppy if he gets dirty.

Vacation Rentals

If you choose to rent a vacation home or condo, the rental agent or owner will give you the details if you are bringing a dog. Self-serve accommodations are also frequently easier when you have a dog than staying in a hotel is. There may be rooms or areas (like furniture) that are off limits to the dog.

Hotels

Some hotels are happy to have your puppy stay in the room and will tell you their own rules on canine conduct that must be observed. Some have designated dog rooms on the ground floor, which means you won't have to carry your puppy or make him climb stairs. Most hotels charge a deposit for pets, refundable upon a room inspection at your checkout.

Do remember:

- Other dogs will already have been in the room, and there may be a risk of fleas.
- Check if there is a designated outdoor potty spot for dogs.
- Most hotels will require that your dog be crated if he is in the room unattended.
- Towels and bathrooms are not provided for the use of the dogs.
- In addition to his crate, take a blanket or bed for your puppy as well as his food and water bowls.

Above: **Teach your puppy to behave around hotels, and follow all rules regarding pets.**

Using Public Places

Public places, such as parks, historical sites, tourist attractions, etc., usually provide information that states whether you are allowed entry with your puppy and whether any areas are restricted. A little research before your take a trip goes a long way in planning your vacation so that you know ahead of time where your pup can and cannot accompany you.

Restaurants

The only dogs allowed inside restaurants are service dogs, but more and more dining establishments are permitting dogs with their owners in outdoor seating areas. A simple Internet search for "dog-friendly restaurants" will turn up several online guides where you can look for such eateries in your area or the area to which you're traveling. If you're not sure if a restaurant allows dogs, be sure to ask first.

Above: **Check before using a dog-friendly beach to see if any areas are designated as off-limits.**

Seaside Vacations

Some seaside resorts may allow dogs on the beaches only at certain (usually off-peak) times of the year. Some beaches have a designated area for dogs and their owners. The best states for beachcombing with your dog are California and Florida, which have the highest concentration of year-round dog-friendly beaches; several others

are located in southern states. No matter what beach you visit, dog droppings are naturally frowned on, so be sure to have bags handy and clean up after your dog. Remember to check your puppy's paws after going on the beach, cleaning out any sand and checking for tar deposits and trapped pieces of shells and pebbles. Bathe or rinse your puppy's coat afterward to remove any salt residue if your puppy has played in the water.

Airline Travel with Your Puppy

Many airlines allow small or young dogs to accompany their owners in the cabin as long as their carriers fit under the seat. Larger dogs must travel as cargo in airline-approved travel crates. This is the general policy followed by most airlines, but each airline's regulations will vary. It's important to check with your airline well in advance and to make sure that your dog is accustomed to the crate in which he will be traveling. The airline will let you know what documentation you need, how the crate is to be labeled, and what to provide for your dog in terms of food and water. Owners of brachycephalic (short-faced) breeds must be aware that some airlines do not allow these dogs

Above: **Most airlines will advise you on the best type of carrier.**

to travel during the summer months, as the heat increases the risk of breathing problems and potentially fatal complications. Owners of dogs that fall under dangerous-dog restrictions may not be able to transport their dogs at all on certain airlines. Check with the airline before you book your tickets.

Above: **Always give your puppy shade to protect him from the sun if you are outside on a hot day.**

Taking Your Puppy Abroad

Taking your dog abroad can be complicated, as each country has specific rules and requirements. Some countries are rabies free, so they need to ensure that pets coming in from abroad will not introduce this disease to their countries. For example, before the introduction of the Pet Travel Scheme (PETS) in the United Kingdom, a six-month quarantine was imposed on all dogs entering from other countries. The best advice for American travelers is to check with the embassy(ies) of the country(ies) to which they are traveling to learn the specific regulations and procedures.

Preventing a Lost Dog

Whether at home with your dog or traveling, there are important safety tips you should follow to ensure your dog's safety and prevent him from getting separated from you.

- If you intend to let your dog off-leash outside, have your yard securely fenced. When not in an enclosed area, keep your dog on leash.
- Teach your dog a reliable "come" command

to prevent his running away should he ever escape his leash, slip through a gate or door, etc.

- Have an ID tag on your dog's collar with your contact information.
- Also have a permanent form of ID, such as a tattoo or a microchip.
- If your dog gets lost, notify local animal control and police right away, as well as those in neighboring towns.

> **Travel Tip**
> If you decide to go on vacation or need to travel with your dog for any reason and he is not already crate-trained, train him to become accustomed to sleeping in a crate well in advance of your trip.

Above: **Micro-chipping a dog is a simple procedure using a special needle, and it can be done from six weeks of age.**

INDEX

PHOTO CREDITS

Bayer HealthCare: 33 left (fleas), 59 bottom right.

Jane Burton, Warren Photographic: Cover (main image), back cover top left, 2, 3, 4, 6 bottom, 10-11, 17, 18 left, 19 bottom, 20 bottom right, 21 top, 21 bottom, 22, 24 top, 26 bottom center, 28 top, 30 center left, 37 top, 38 (all three), 42 bottom, 44 top, 44 center left, 45 bottom, 46 (both), 47 top, 51 bottom, 53 bottom left.

Dreamstime.com:
Ellah Hanochi: 8 bottom right.
Elliot Westacott: 1.

Interpet Archive: 12 bottom left, 13 top right, 13 bottom left, 16 center right, 29 left, 36 bottom left and right, 37 center left, 40 bottom, 43 top left, 45 center left, 45 top right, 48 top, 49 top, 50 bottom, 50-51 (sequence), 56 top.

iStockphoto.com:
Vyacheslav Anyakin: 23 bottom (meat).
Christine Balderas: 12 top right.
Dana Bartekoske: 31 top.
Maria Bibikova: 56 bottom.
Joshua Blake: 25 bottom.
Aleksander Bochenek: 58 left.
Dan Brandenburg: 7 left.
Anna Bryukanova: 7 top right.
Steven Dern: 35 top left.
Doctor_Bass: 53 center right.
Stacey Gamez: 40 top.
Robyn Glover: 15 top right.
Anna Grzelewska: 16 top left.
Memet Salih Guler: 42 top.
Simon Gurney: 57 bottom.
Jasna Hrovatin: 59 top.
Eric Isselée: 5 top, 5 middle, 6 top, 11 top right (dog), 27 top, 54.
Matthew Jacques: 24 bottom.
Jeridu: 33 center.
Verity Johnson: Back cover top right, 39, 47 center right.

Eric Lam: Back cover bottom right, 5 bottom, 15 top left, 41, 49 bottom.
Zsolt Langviser: 14 center right.
Warwick Lister-Kaye: 28 bottom.
Sean Locke: 26 bottom right.
Valerie Loiseleux: 11 top (cup).
Gina Luck: 43 top right.
Pamela Moore: 25 top.
Valentin Mosichev: 23 bottom (tomatoes).
Günay Mutlu: 48 bottom.
Marilyn Nieves: 35 bottom.
Lynn Paukovitch: 35 center right.
Monique Rodriguez: 34.
Leigh Schindler: 20 top, 30 bottom.
Evgeny Shevchenko: 20 bottom left.
Nick Tzolov: 37 bottom.
Lisa F. Young: 8 top left.
Zts: 23 bottom (carrots).

Alun John: 55, 57 top.

Merial Animal Health Ltd: 33 right (mites).

Photos.com: Jupiterimages Corporation: Back cover center right

Shutterstock Inc.:
Afarland: 53 top left.
Annette: 12 center left.
John Bell: 52.
Joy Brown: 9 top.
Cameron Cross: 58 right.
Elnur: 8 top.
Eric Isselée: 10 top left, 29 top right.
Wendy Kaveny Photography: 31 bottom.
Anne Kitzman: 18 top.
Paul Krugloff: 23 (wet food).
Emin Ozkan: 16 top.
David Scheuber: 43 bottom.
April Turner: 23 (puppy and bowl), 23 (dried food).
Wojciech Zbieg: 9 bottom.

Case: Front cover, Ron Kimball/www.kimball stock.com, Warren Photographic (all other images).